African Grey
Parrot
Handbook

Mattie Sue Athan
and Dianalee Deter

BARRON'S

Dedication

To Sam, Noreen, and Larry, for their unfailing love and support.

All inquiries should be addressed to:
Barron's Educational Series, Inc.
250 Wireless Boulevard
Hauppauge, New York 11788
www.barronseduc.com

Library of Congress Catalog Card No. 2008051511

ISBN-13: 978-0-7641-4140-9
ISBN-10: 0-7641-4140-6

Library of Congress Cataloging-in-Publication Data
Athan, Mattie Sue.
   The African grey parrot handbook / Mattie Sue Athan and Dianalee Deter ; drawings by Michele Earle-Bridges.
—2nd ed.
      p.   cm.
   Includes index.
   ISBN-13: 978-0-7641-4140-9
   ISBN-10: 0-7641-4140-6
   1. African grey parrot. I. Deter, Dianalee. II. Title.

SF473.P3A8365   2009
636.6'865—dc22   2008051511

Printed in China

9 8 7 6 5 4

About the Authors

Mattie Sue Athan is one of the world's most experienced parrot behavior consultants. Having studied her craft since 1978, her area of special interest is the development of independence. Her first book, *Guide to a Well-Behaved Parrot* won Amazon.com's bestselling bird care book award. Her sixth book, *Parrots: A Complete Pet Owner's Manual*, won the Oklahoma Writers' Federation Best Non-Fiction Book Award.

Dianalee Deter has a bachelor of science degree in zoology from the University of Florida. She began working with parrots in 1986, and is a noted expert. She is the co-author of *Guide to the Senegal Parrot and Its Family*, also published by Barron's.

Photo Credits

Mattie Sue Athan: page 52; Joan Balzarini: pages viii, 4, 7, 11, 13, 15, 17, 20, 22, 35, 36, 43, 45, 48, 59, 61, 62, 64, 67, 69, 72, 82, 85, 87, 93, 95, 99, 104, 109, 114, 125, 134, 145, 152, 157; Dianalee Deter: page 90; Isabelle Francais: pages vii, 3, 5, 8, 19, 31, 39, 40, 46, 51, 54, 55, 56, 68, 70, 74, 78, 81, 88, 92, 96, 100, 101, 102, 103, 106, 116, 118, 121, 127, 132, 136, 142, 147; Pet Profiles: pages 98, 113; Susan Green: page 25.

Cover Credits

Shutterstock: front cover, back cover, inside back cover, inside front cover.

Contents

Preface

It has been nearly a decade since the first edition of this book was published. The world has changed in ways we never could have imagined, and language has changed along with it. The authors of this book have enjoyed eighteen more combined years of observing African grey parrots, almost doubling our experience to half a century. We've learned better ways to describe those observations, and we've had more opportunities to practice merging our different perspectives.

Expect this book to be the same practical, dependable resource for living with greys but better organized and an easier read than the first edition. While we've included as much scientific data as possible, most of the information here reflects hands-on experience. African greys—especially handfeds—can be more sensitive than most other common companion parrots. You will see technqiues, observations, and strategies here that differ from those used to modify behavior in other types of parrots.

Much of the first edition was obviously "new territory," as we included issues and behaviors that had not been previously discussed in print, but don't expect this to be the last you'll hear from us on grey parrots. As with the first edition, this book will be expanded and updated as new information becomes available. We'd like to thank our editor, Dave Rodman, and everyone who helped us in our quest to understand the African grey parrot.

Chapter One

The Grey Parrot Chronicles

Somewhere far from the jungle, the companion parrot enjoys a sheltered indoor existence with humans, developing both communication and cooperation skills while pursuing its very own "agenda." Centuries before New World parrots were known to exist, African greys staked out this shared indoor territory, enjoying (or suffering from) great popularity even in ancient Rome. In spite of this long history, the bird's genetic programming can make living with an African grey parrot more like sharing a home with a wild child, roommate, or rival than a pet.

The larger subspecies, *Psittacus erithacus erithacus,* and the smaller Timneh African grey parrot *(Psittacus erithacus Timneh)* are numerous in captivity even as their numbers decline in the wild. Both subspecies are predominantly grey with lighter scalloping on the feathers of the head and neck. The eyes of both birds are silvery yellow, usually pale, but sometimes bright. *Erithacus erithacus,* the larger bird, has a distinct red tail and a solid black beak and will be called herein "Congo" or Red-tailed grey. The smaller bird will be called the Timneh. In intelligence, behavior, talking abililty, and numerous other traits—excepting appearance—the two subspecies are similar, or even sometimes identical, unless noted. Both subspecies bear powder on the feathers, not unlike, but to a lesser extent, than cockatoos. Opportunistic omnivores, these parrots' bare face patches probably evolved to enable them to consume anything, perhaps even carrion when necessary, without retaining rotten tidbits on their feathers after eating.

Individual Red-tailed birds occur in significant color variations, which may be light silver or almost black depending upon the point of origin of their ancestors. Some individual Congos exhibit slight color variations by gender, however; ambiguous and crossover coloration occur frequently, especially among birds with different ancestry, and DNA analysis rather than markings remains the best way to determine gender. Both subspecies possess equal talking abilities, with some individuals exhibiting exceptional mimicking and communication skills.

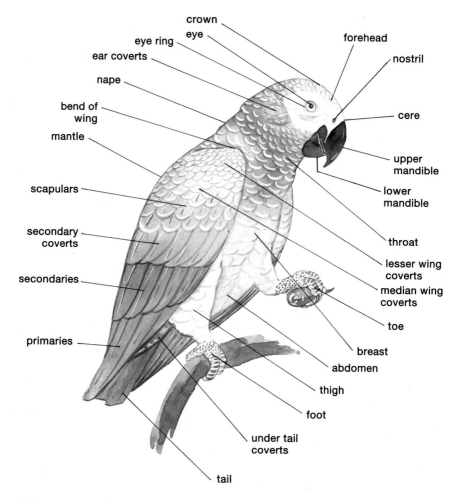

crown
eye ring
eye
ear coverts
nape
bend of
wing
mantle
scapulars
secondary
coverts
secondaries
primaries
forehead
nostril
cere
upper
mandible
lower
mandible
throat
lesser wing
coverts
median wing
coverts
toe
breast
abdomen
thigh
foot
under tail
coverts
tail

African grey parrot anatomy.

The tail of the Timneh has a brown-ish wash over red, sometimes giving it a maroon appearance, sometimes reddish brown. The Timneh has a black-tipped, dark rosy-pink or horn-colored upper beak and a solid black lower beak. The iris may be more sil-ver than yellow. The captive-raised Timneh may be more active and behaviorally stolid than the Red-tailed grey. Timnehs may learn human words earlier than Congos and may be more inclined to talk in the pres-ence of strangers. In our experience, Timnehs appear to have less tendency to develop both ongoing fearfulness and feather-chewing disorders than the Red-tailed African grey.

Grey Parrots in Africa

Grey parrots commonly inhabit lowland forests, although they often visit open land adjacent to woodlands. They go to the ground with caution, circling a clearing sometimes twice before landing. They are known to pick up quartz from the ground[1] and go to the ground to drink at elephant wallows and pathways.[2] Wild grey parrots are extremely shy and rarely allow humans to approach.

The wild grey's native diet includes mostly high-occurring fruits such as oil-palm (Elaeis guinensis) nuts, other nuts, seeds, fruits, and berries. They are famous for damaging maize crops. When they can be seen, grey parrots are often observed carrying oil-palm nuts and other prized foods long distances before consuming them.

The birds roost in large groups, often calling loudly morning and evening and in flight. Flocks are described as very noisy. Greys may roost in trees over water, even preferring roosting on islands in rivers. Flocking behavior is most often reported outside breeding season.

Most nesting is probably solitary, although greys have been seen nesting in large groups with only one pair per tree. Wolfgang de Graul reports that offspring are usually produced during or just after the rainy season.[3] Tony Juniper and Mike Parr suggest that breeding season varies with locale and that dry season breeding is common in some areas.[4] De Graul also reports that "...nesting trees inherited by those born in them once existed and perhaps still do in certain areas...."

As the need for human habitat grows, grey parrots decline in the wild. Comparing charts of the grey parrots' range between 1976 (de Graul) and 1998 (Juniper and Parr) the birds appear to have lost habitat on the northern and southern reaches of the range and expanded with agriculture to the east.

Although grey parrots were the second most heavily traded parrot in the world in the 1980s, they are still common where large tracts of forest remain and are still numerous in some areas, especially in the Congo

basin rain forests. Habitat loss in some parts of their range, including Nigeria to Sierra Leone, and extensive trapping have lead to population declines, especially around towns and cities.[5] In the past, natives sold greys and often even hand-fed and trained them. However, they did not keep them as pets. Legal importation of grey parrots into the United States ended in 1992. Grey parrots are still legally trapped and exported from some parts of Africa to countries not yet participating in the Convention on International Trade in Endangered Species.

Grey Parrots Indoors

A companion grey is not a pet. It's an exotic, undomesticated animal that exhibits instinctual wild charac- teristics, especially instinctual behaviors related to reproduction that do not usually appear in (spayed or neutered) pet dogs and cats. Although young parrots often exhibit behaviors that seem to be motivated by a desire to please, these behaviors are actually motivated by a desire to belong to a flock, as this means safety. As the bird matures, its behaviors will become increasingly independent. As with dogs and horses, early and ongoing behavior training can redirect the development of unwelcome instinctual behaviors as the birds mature. Without ongoing behavioral support, many, possibly most, companion grey parrots can easily revert to destructive wild behaviors or will adapt some unwanted behaviors to replace wild ones. Some wild behaviors fit in well in the living room environment; some do not. Since grey parrots live such a long time—up to 50 years—the acquisition of only one difficult-to-live-with behavior every year or two can produce an obnoxious bird by the time it's a teenager.

Today's companion greys are, at most, two generations out of the wild. The behaviors they improvise are generated by instincts that enabled their ancestors to survive in the wild. The wild parrot lived, loved, learned, and evolved through thousands of generations in order to have the skills necessary to meet nature's challenges. Wild parrots must learn a diverse assortment of transportation and communication skills; they must know how to find and separate good food from toxic plants; they must know how to defend territory, how to recognize and avoid predators, how to find safe water, and how to rejoin their families when separated. They must be able to do all this sometimes in blinding rain or oppressive drought. They must face the challenges of finding and keeping a mate alive, of developing role-appropriate behaviors, of competing for and defending nesting sites, and of creating, nurturing, and teaching their extremely helpless offspring to do the same. They must have some mechanism by which to evaluate the food supply in order to determine whether a nesting process should be completed.

A very different set of behaviors are necessary for life in the living room.

Almonds and other nuts from trees are safer than peanuts (legumes).

The Fully Weaned Juvenile

A premium hand-fed baby grey should be weaned completely before going to its new home. While there is no magical age at which this happens, it usually occurs some time between four and seven months of age. Some birds may take more time, but rarely less time, to be physically and emotionally weaned. Birds that have been allowed to fully fledge (fly) will usually develop the confidence necessary to successfully change homes earlier.

There is a window-of-opportunity of about eight to ten weeks after

weaning during which the bird will willingly change role models (flock/home). This is probably about the time the bird would first begin interacting with other parrots outside its immediate family of parents and siblings. Most breeder/dealers prefer to sell greys during this window. A grey parrot over nine months old may be reluctant to change a parent-baby bond and too young to abandon that bond for a more mature bond. These birds can usually go easily and successfully to new homes during or after they have completed their first wing feather molt at 12 to 18 months.

Training social behaviors is best begun even before the bird goes to its new home, and carefully continued in the new home. Another window-of-opportunity opens for teaching a young grey both human-interactive behaviors and independence. In the wild, the young bird would be learning important skills during this time. Its brain will be quickly filled with all the information needed to live. This is probably the most important developmental period in the bird's life, for if appropriate skills are not learned at this time, the wild bird will not survive.

If the physical or behavioral environment is inappropriate during these early days in the home, then a grey parrot can become uncooperative, shy, excessively vocal, or over-bonded to a particular individual to the exclusion of others.

Companion greys must learn cooperation, acceptance of change, and independent play in order to fully enjoy sharing life with people. These behaviors develop with consistent handling, redundant patterning, and sensitive environmental manipulations as described in this book and in *Parrots, Guide to a Well-Behaved Parrot*, and *Guide to Companion Parrot Behavior*, both by the co-author of this book, Mattie Sue Athan. While tendencies toward aggression are expected and usually considered somewhat "normal," developing fearfulness must be treated immediately, for this can lead to unwelcome stress reactions.

Expect to raise a baby grey almost exactly as you treat a child. Never punish the bird, especially by hitting, squirting, or dropping. Even "the evil eye" and "time-outs" can be frightening for an extremely sensitive grey. An African grey is an undomesticated animal, and it may respond to perceived violence as though it feared for its life.

The "Honeymoon"

The bird must be patterned to appropriate behaviors by example and reward, practice and repetition. Fortunately, this is usually easily accomplished in a properly weaned, normally experimental, well-socialized hand-fed juvenile grey. During the first three to six months in the home, a hand-fed grey should be curious and eager to please. This is the juvenile developmental period sometimes called "the honeymoon period," a time during which confidence gradually turns from approval seeking to independence and the instinct to control. Possibly because of their extreme intelligence, grey parrots can develop a surprising diversity of both wanted and unwanted behaviors.

There's a very real temptation to believe that because a weaned juvenile grey parrot is "perfect" when it comes home, it will stay that way. The dependent baby will mature into a creature that strives to be a productive member of the flock. Left undirected, these activities include chewing nest sites and foraging areas, such as furniture or computer parts, calling the "flock"—screaming when the owner leaves the room, joining in vocal social interactions—outtalking the telephone or TV, and allopreening—removing moles or jewelry. Without planning or behavior training, grey parrots can easily develop a wide range of behaviors that don't contribute either to a happy life or to good behavioral adjustment.

Language and Its Use

Like other intelligent species—such as humans, chimpanzees, elephants, whales—the baby grey's intellectual and behavioral development requires a relatively long time. Juvenile greys are not considered emotionally and behaviorally independent until approximately two

Unweaned babies can be recognized by their large crops—food pouches between the beaks and chests.

Not Forgotten

For many years, Dr. Irene Pepperberg has studied and statistically analyzed the African grey parrot's speaking abilities. Working first with Alex, who was lost to heart disease at the age of 30, Dr. Pepperberg evaluated the African grey's abilities to answer questions about familiar objects, their shape, number, substance, and color. Dr. Pepperberg didn't only evaluate talking; she also documented methods by which birds acquire human speech. Especially, she has observed that grey parrots learn best when competing against a rival. Dr. Pepperberg's most famous study used competition to stimulate language acquisition and use.

years of age. This is especially noticeable in the development of talking skills. Even compared with other parrots, human words are learned a little more slowly by greys.

Parrots have no vocal cords. Sounds are produced when air is forced across the top of the trachea, a process that resembles blowing across the top of a soda bottle. Variations in pitch and volume are produced when the bird changes the shape of the trachea. This requires practice. A baby grey rehearses quietly, muttering softly, until it is confident enough to loudly produce the sounds it likes. While a particular baby parrot might learn a few words before it is weaned, many greys may not be understandable until about 11 months.

The African grey parrot must be protected from learning unpleasant human sounds such as squeals, squeaks, screeches, burps, belches, and worse. The bird must also be protected from learning profanity, for it will probably outlive humans in the household and will say in its next home what it heard in the first. Greys must also be protected from learning the screams of other parrots and barking from dogs, as they may repeat these sounds frequently and with great relish.

Cooperation Exercises

A successful companion grey should be both cooperative and independent. A hand-fed bird first learns cooperation by being fed by humans. The weaned juvenile should be able to expect that food and water will always be available. How, then, are cooperation skills generated and reinforced after weaning?

From its first days in the home, the baby grey should enjoy practicing the step-up routine for at least a minute or two most days. The bird's enjoyment of the process is a very necessary part of this interaction. Unless a bird is cooperative enough and well patterned enough to step up from an unfamiliar perch in unfamiliar territory, it may refuse to step up from the cage or other familiar perch. Step-up practice may initially have to take place outside the bird's established territory. A laundry room or hallway is usually perfect, as the bird will probably never spend much time in these areas, and therefore should not develop territorial behav-

ior there. A cooperative bird can be successfully patterned anywhere it feels safe. Good behavioral strategies for the future include practice stepping up the bird:

1. from the hand to and from an unfamiliar perch;

2. from hand to hand;

3. from a hand-held perch to and from an unfamiliar perch;

4. from a hand-held perch to a hand-held perch;

5. from a familiar perch to and from both hands and to and from hand-held perches.

Be sure to reward the bird after each completed step up. Warm, genuine human enthusiasm is an excellent reward for the bird's success in stepping up, but affection rewards work well only if the bird likes the trainer. Use food rewards for successful step ups if the bird is to be handled by multiple individuals.

Like other effective behavioral strategies, step ups must be practiced consistently and sensitively. Step-up practice inspires, facilitates, and habituates cooperation in a baby parrot. The predictability of human and bird responses to one another provides a comfortable standard for all other interactions. Each human expecting to interact with the bird should practice step ups most days for a minute or so and in a routine variety of ways. Especially with shy or cautious birds, as many grey parrots are, the bird's enjoyment of the process is absolutely necessary.

If the command is not successful, technique, approach, or prompting mannerisms must be altered. Do not continue with unsuccessful methods. Be careful not to reinforce unsuccessful patterns. If the bird is not eagerly, or at least willingly, cooperating with step ups and step-up practice, something is wrong, and you should seek professional help.

An effective relationship with a grey must begin with and maintain both mutual trust and respect. If bird and humans achieve no mutual respect, the relationship is lost. If, for example, the baby parrot begins to treat a human like a piece of property rather than a respected flockmate, everybody could be in trouble. Although most grey parrots go through a nippy stage—this is part of the normal development of independence and personality in many juvenile hookbills—the appearance of biting behaviors around a particular person or location can signal the development of territorial or bonding-related aggression.

Frequent, exciting, and/or soothing verbal reinforcement are necessary components of successful step-up practice. Reinforcing the bird to enjoy step-up practice not only acts to prevent the development of aggression, but also prevents the occasional development of shyness. While an aggressive juvenile parrot gains cooperation skills from step ups, the shy or fearful bird can learn confidence from the joy and predictability of the interaction.

Early patterning is also necessary to prevent the development of stress reactions to toweling. A companion parrot requires annual veterinary examinations and grooming at least twice yearly. Cuddling, snuggling, and playing "peek-a-bird" in a towel will improve trust and condition the baby to be more tolerant of being restrained during these potentially stressful interactions.

We must be empathetic and predictable in the handling of all baby parrots, but the maintenance of trust is especially important to the greys. These birds sometimes tend to exhibit extreme responses. Red-tails and, to a lesser extent, Timnehs, have an occasional tendency to suddenly acquire surprising fearful behaviors. Use extra care and consistency with grey parrots to compensate for this sensitivity.

Bonding and Socialization

In order to maintain an interactive disposition, it's important to avoid allowing a grey parrot to become overly possessive of a particular human or territory. The bird should have relationships with many humans and other safe animals, and should spend as much time as possible in diverse locations inside and out of the home. Early socialization to enjoy changes in the cage and home environment, access to appropriate choices, and bird-safe outings to meet sensitive, interactive humans will acclimate the bird to tolerate the inevitable twists of fate that plague all creatures.

Chewing and Messiness

Grey parrots are cavity breeders; they lay eggs and raise babies in hollowed out, mostly wooden spaces. When a cavity-breeding parrot is gleefully turning the priceless antique clock into toothpicks, it's really saying, "Look how sexy I am! I would be a fantastic mate. I could make a nice big nest cavity for you and our babies."

Providing a grey with appropriate chewables will help save the furniture and woodwork. Providing for chewing behaviors will help to prevent biting, excessive vocalization, nail biting, overpreening, feather chewing, and other innovated displacement behaviors.

Chewing and its ugly cousin, messiness, are innate behaviors, not behavior problems. They must be accepted and accommodated because they are part of the parrot's nature that cannot be changed. A good-quality cage is especially important here. The cage may be the most significant factor in whether or not the bird succeeds in its first home. A hard-to-clean cage can easily inspire resentment in humans responsible for cleaning and can damage the human/bird bond.

Interacting vocally is an important part of bonding with the flock. Vocal behaviors—babbling or talking—can develop almost any time before or after weaning. Grey parrot vocalization might include some annoying

whistles but will probably not include screaming. While these interactive behaviors stimulate talking, they can turn into irritating, attention-demanding noises. Independent play must be encouraged by providing interesting tools (toys).

Appropriate human behavior also contributes to appropriate behavior in companion greys. If humans in the household demonstrate play and communication skills in constructive ways, the grey parrot will likely do likewise. That is, if humans use screaming, domination, and force in their interactions with the bird, it will likely do the same. It might also develop fearful responses.

Would You Enjoy a Grey Companion?

Grey parrots have a reputation for extreme intelligence, ability to repeat words and sounds, and to use them with understanding. These sturdy birds reproduce readily in captivity and are usually available almost any place parrots are commonly kept. As companions they easily command a respected position in the human household. They can be expensive and long lived.

A grey parrot is a wild (undomesticated) animal and not necessarily a perfect companion for every human. The bird must be trained to cooperate, guided to emotional independence, and accommodated for its natural behaviors. If you love planning, playing chess, and other forms of strategy, you would probably love a grey. If you think you could tolerate an occasional temper tantrum and are willing to put up with some damaged possessions and mess in order to share the company of sublime feathered joy, then a grey parrot might be perfect for you.

Potential behavioral issues discussed here are usually easily prevented. A new grey parrot owner who applies the principles set forth in this book might never see *any* unexpected behavior.

[1]Joseph M. Forshaw, *Parrots of the World*. T.F.H. Publications, 1978, pp. 287–288.
[2]Parrot's: Look Who's Talking. Thirteen/WNET and BBC-TV, Video, 1995.
[3]Wolfgang de Graul, *The Grey Parrot.* T.F.H. Publications, 1987.
[4]Juniper, Tony, and Mike Parr. *Parrots, a Guide to Parrots of the World.* Yale University Press, New Haven and London, 1998, pp. 375–376.
[5]Ibid., 376.

Chapter Two

Going Grey

Since the start a baby grey parrot receives affects its longevity and quality of life as a companion to humans, it's best to decide *where* to get the bird before selecting one. Carefully consider potential sources so that you are confident that the needs of the bird—as well as your own—will be met.

- Before going home, the baby must be fully weaned onto a healthy diet.
- The bird should be well acclimated to its own cage and responding curiously to toys.
- If wing feathers are to be trimmed, the young bird will have a better sense of confidence if it has been allowed to learn to fly.
- Leave wings and nails as long as possible so that the bird retains balance and gripping skills.
- Expect a written health guarantee of at least a week after taking the baby home.
- Expect a conscientious seller to provide easy access to information about care and training.

Dealers who are most careful about the quality of homes their babies go into are likely to have done a thorough and effective job all around, including crucial early socialization and weaning. Many aviaries require an appointment to see birds. Some require applications from potential owners and strict requirements that new owners have to meet. Some breeders now require that new parrot owners attend classes before being allowed to take a bird home.

When considering neonates, follow the breeder's handling instructions precisely, as the babies are

Peeking Out

When fluff-covered baby greys aren't sleeping or scratching in corners, they like to stretch their long necks to see over the sides of their containers. Big black eyes and soft whimpers are an unmistakable invitation to pick them up and cuddle. When a willing human stops by for snuggling, the little birds make it more than obvious how appreciated the attention is. Neonatal (unweaned) baby greys have a way of melting human hearts; therefore, it is best not to pick up a baby grey while holding a credit card until other details have been determined.

best handled in familiar ways: After carefully washing your hands, talk softly and move carefully; play eye games. Once they are moving around well, baby greys should start responding by turning toward the person talking and by answering back. Sometimes the babies come running over, but this depends on how many strangers they've seen recently. Avoid babies that stay cowered in the corner, fearing interaction.

Newly weaned juveniles still have black eyes that later fade to gray and finally turn variable shades of yellow by the time the bird is two years old. While some individuals' eyes change quickly and some do not, if the eyes are not yet yellow, the bird is still very young. Baby Congos have black on the edges of tail feathers. Baby Timnehs' tail feathers are often almost completely black.

When considering a neonatal (unweaned) or juvenile grey, be respectful because of your unfamiliar status. A content young grey may not want to come off a familiar perch or out of a cage to be with a stranger. It's better if someone known to the bird picks it up and hands it to a newcomer. Avoid birds that jump to the floor or the bottom of the cage growling when approached.

Initial interactions should be vocal and passive. Avoid putting fingers where the parrot might be tempted to bite them. The bird should look comfortable on a stranger's hand, but it is sometimes too much to ask to pet a grey parrot right away. If the

bird has been well raised, it is happy and secure where it is and has no reason to look for alternatives. This doesn't mean the bird will not bond; it's a sign of a well-developed sense of security. The bird will be well adjusted when it does bond.

Evaluating the Chick

In addition to evaluating whether the bird has a good emotional and behavioral start, a prospective owner should perform a careful physical examination before deciding whether or not to buy a particular bird.

- Fluffy neonates should be plump and round. Fledging greys may seem a little thin, but not skinny. You should be able to feel, but not see, the breastbone. Muscles on each side of the breastbone should feel firm and well fleshed.
- Eyes should be clear and black, round and watchful. The eyes will begin to change color after about four months. Some individuals may have silver eyes by the time they are seven or eight months old; others may have gray eyes for over 18 months. This may be gender-related, with males' eyes changing faster.
- Nares (nostrils) should be clear of discharge. Breathing should be easy and uniform with no audible click.
- Beak should be straight and smooth. There should be no noticeable ridges on the exterior surface. Both Red-tails and Timnehs will have black beaks as neonates.
- Feathers may have some baby food stuck to them, as the powder down that helps them keep feathers clean has not yet come in.
- Juvenile coloring such as black on tails or red spots on thighs or breast may be apparent.
- Feet should open and close with two toes pointing forward and two toes pointing back. Toes should be straight with sharp nails and no swollen joints or sores on the bottoms of the feet.
- There should be no feces caked around the vent.

Shoppers' Etiquette

1. Don't risk carrying disease from one place to another. Bathe and change clothes and shoes between each store or aviary visited.

2. Politely observe house rules for handling baby birds, which may include asking first to handle a baby, washing or disinfecting your hands, and stepping through disinfectant to minimize possible disease transmission.

3. Don't provoke the birds by waving fingers in their faces.

- Droppings may have a lot of water since hand-feeding formulas are high in moisture, but all three parts, feces, urates, and urine, should be present and well formed.
- Don't be concerned about occasional stress bars across the wing or tail feathers, but be wary of a bird with multiple stress bars on each feather, which might be an indication that it has been ill.
- Feathers should be uniformly shaped. The sheath of unopened developing feathers should be pointed and not rounded on the tips before the feather opens. Undeveloped feathers should be well attached and not easily bumped out by normal petting, as this could be a sign of illness. Mature birds should have powder on the feathers.
- The breeder should tell you if the youngster has been treated by a veterinarian for illness. This does

not indicate that the bird is "sickly." Baby birds and elderly birds are the most susceptible to illness. There should be a health guarantee so that you can be assured by any veterinarian that the baby is healthy at the time it is taken to its new home.

Bond and Switch

In the past, it was sometimes presumed that for each owner, personally hand-feeding his or her own bird was the best way to develop a strong bond with a companion parrot. This advice has led to many disappointments. Removing a baby from its parent during the most precarious learning situation undermines confidence. Additionally, many baby birds that were so carefully hand-fed, with all the worry and angst involved, switched bonds later. Any parrot will avoid forming a mate bond with its parent. The bird forms a parent/offspring bond with the hand-feeder/parent and flock member bonds in the new home.

We can't say this enough: The consequences of successfully weaning a grey are so dire that it should be left only to experienced professionals with all the resources necessary—including other grey parrots—to produce an exploratory, confident, interactive, and independent parrot.

Grapes are wonderful treats or rewards, but are high in sugar and have limited nutritional value.

Food and Related Issues

African greys are famous and dedicated eaters. In a flock of mixed species, hand-fed parrots, the grey is the one with its face most often hidden in the food dish. Some juveniles spend so much time in the food dish that passersby might be prompted to ask if there is something wrong with the bird. Every piece of food will be chewed and sucked dry so that it looks like it went through a food processor and was then dehydrated.

Allowing this interaction with food is important in the bird's development. An appropriate hand-feeding method allows the bird to experience food going into its mouth and down its throat. Early exposure to

the tastes and textures of food provides the young parrot with important information and stimulation. Solid food should be available to the baby well before weaning.

A properly weaned juvenile grey should have had experience with a variety of healthy food items. The new owner should not have to put the new bird through the stresses of a diet change when bringing it home. The new parrot is best off if it is required to tolerate as few major changes as possible—and that includes diet.

Weaning, Confidence, and Constructive Interactions

African grey parrots, especially Congos, can develop problematic behaviors such as feather chewing, fear reactions, shrieking, and repetitive/compulsive behaviors. Compassionate humans work hard to prevent these unsavory developments by providing for all their birds' needs in a timely manner. A suitable, well-positioned cage, easily gripped perches, a variety of toys, a diverse, nutritious diet, regular attention, appropriate grooming, and opportunities for exercise can fill the needs of most companion birds. However, some greys that appear to have an ideal life with every possible need provided still

Beyond Weaning

Of course, juvenile greys should not go to their new homes before being fully weaned, but a few other considerations are important as well. While with other types of parrots the ability to eat solid food on their own is associated with independence, greys need a little more. Once a baby grey has flown and is eating on its own, it then begins, under the supervision of its trusted "parent," to learn survival skills. For companion greys, this means exploring, playing with toys, vocalizing, and otherwise interacting. A baby grey, removed from its "parent" too soon can be emotionally vulnerable. Promote confidence by allowing the little bird to stay with its human hand-feeder until at least 16 weeks of age. For many greys, the time should be longer (the bird is considered juvenile until it is 18 to 24 months old).

may occasionally develop neurotic behaviors, especially shredding, clipping, or pulling feathers. Many of these neurotic behaviors can be traced to failure to develop independence as a juvenile.

A neonatal grey can be an intensely needy bird. An Amazon of comparable age might call when it's hungry, then go back to sleep when fed. However, a hand-feeding baby grey might call for attention even though it is already fed and not yet hungry. A baby grey needs the reassurance of touch, to have its head rubbed, and to be snuggled. Greys often do much better if they are not raised alone and have another bird to cuddle with and preen. Many breeders and hand-feeders give an "only chick" grey a safe stuffed animal to provide the physical and emotional support usually provided by a clutch mate.

Once the bird is covered with feathers, snuggling should give way to playing and learning. This is the perfect time to begin combining snuggling and playing peek-a-boo in a towel. This snuggling exercise, called the "towel game," will be used later to provide an immediate sense of safety anytime it's needed.

As the baby bird matures, it more readily shows curiosity and playfulness if it has a strong connection with its parent/hand-feeder and receives regular attention. Many people are worried that giving a young bird too much attention results in a "spoiled" bird that constantly demands attention. In most cases, however, it is not possible to give a baby grey too much attention, as long as much of that attention is constructive interaction such as playing games, engaging in enjoyable patterning routines, or modeling appropriate behaviors—and as long as the bird has adequate time alone to develop independent toy play.

At this time, the juvenile grey will be driven to copy the actions of an adult or of a perceived parent. The young bird requires a role model to follow and it derives security from

being able to fill this need. The person playing the parent bird role must spend a lot of time actively involved in the bird's quest for knowledge. The baby grey will instinctively trust the acting "parent" to teach it and will be more open to the person who accepts that role.

The more time spent helping the bird to develop a sense of curiosity, the more likely that the bird will be interested in new situations rather than being afraid of them. The more foods that are introduced to the youngster by its role model, the greater variety of foods the bird will willingly try later. The hand-feeder must teach the bird about food and toys and should allow the juvenile bird to develop observable confidence before sending it off to join a new "flock."

Transition to the New Home

Wing feathers: Before bringing the weaned juvenile parrot home, ask the breeder or dealer to see that the bird's wing feathers are properly trimmed. For a grey, this means leaving enough feathers to allow safe gliding. Outside, a breeze can turn gliding into flying. A newly purchased juvenile grey does not belong outdoors unless it's in a cage or carrier.

Temperature: Find out what temperature the bird is accustomed to. If the weather is cold, warm up the car before taking the baby outside. Carry the bird in a rigid carrier that can be covered on the outside and can be belted into the car for safety. A mature companion grey can happily tolerate much cooler temperatures than most humans, but this is a baby grey enduring the stress of changing homes. For the first week or so, it's a good idea to keep the newly acquired juvenile a little warmer (about five degrees) than the usual anticipated room temperature.

Quarantine: Carefully quarantine the new bird to make sure it has no contact with any other birds in the home until the veterinarian says such interaction is not dangerous. Most veterinarians will probably rec-

ommend a quarantine period of at least 30 days.

Avian veterinarians: A responsible dealer will give a reasonable guarantee of the bird's health, but you should take the bird as soon as possible to an experienced avian veterinarian for any tests the veterinarian recommends. If the bird is not at least 16 weeks old, its immune system is not fully developed, and extra precautions must be taken. Try to schedule the veterinarian's first appointment in the morning so that the baby won't be exposed to dust from other birds. If possible, take the baby in its own cage and cover the outside bottom of the cage or carrier with a plastic garbage bag so that it won't leave or pick up germs when it is set down in the veterinarian's facility.

The veterinarian might suggest DNA testing to determine gender. Expect the veterinarian to recommend laboratory tests to verify the bird's health, including a test for PBFD. The costs of diagnostic tests are not usually part of the bird's health guarantee from the seller, but they could save much expense and heartache later if the baby bird turns out to be harboring an unseen illness or disease. If diagnostic tests determine that the bird has a health problem, a responsible dealer honoring a guarantee will provide treatment. Some dealers will expect the bird to be returned for treatment or to be treated by the veterinarian they choose.

Bands: A loose-fitting band can be dangerous. Ask the veterinarian whether or not the bird's band fits properly or whether it should be removed. A bird without a band can have its DNA registered for identification purposes. Some veterinarians might suggest microchipping. We favor DNA registry for grey parrots because of occasional apparent adverse reactions to microchipping.

Stress Management

Avoid as much stress as possible when relocating a parrot. Changing too many of the things that are important to the parrot can undermine the sense of security of even the most confident grey parrot. Ideally, the bird should go to its new home in a familiar cage with familiar toys to be fed familiar food by familiar people.

An Appropriate Cage

Provide an appropriate cage while waiting for the neonate to wean. This way the baby can grow up in the cage it will occupy as a juvenile and will feel more secure in any surroundings. If the bird is already weaned and ready to go, the new caregiver should try to provide a cage as similar as possible to the one the bird has been living in. Or, the bird might be introduced to a new cage at least a week or two before leaving the place it knows. Again, beloved and familiar toys should be moved with the bird.

Fear Response

During these early weeks and months, the juvenile grey develops its view of the world. A bird that sees its environment as scary and unpredictable can quickly develop a fear response to anything unfamiliar. While these fear responses might serve the grey parrot well in the wild, where predators are waiting at every turn, these same fear responses are problematic in companion parrots. A young grey that has been carefully protected and nurtured through this time will be a more stable bird that will more easily weather the changes that occur naturally in life.

1. Try to bring the juvenile grey home as early as possible during the day so that the bird can become accustomed to its surroundings before dark.

2. Keep a towel over about half of the cage for the first few days.

3. Provide a small night-light, especially if there are pets in the home that might move around in the dark. A bird that is disturbed at night and not getting enough sleep will be physically and emotionally stressed. Consider the possibility of a separate place to sleep.

4. Warm foods such as oatmeal, cooked squash, or sweet potatoes can be very comforting to a newly weaned juvenile grey. In addition to offering the same diet it was on before coming into your home, offering warm "comfort foods" daily for a while will help provide a smooth transition to the new home, and most African greys will enjoy warm treats occasionally throughout their lives.

Early Education

Most of the strategies that African greys use to get along in life are learned. Communicating, eating, toy play, and learning what to be afraid of all contribute to the development of independence. Many other types of parrots are independent by nature; companion greys learn independence

Gradual Transition

There should be a gradual transition between the perceived constant attention from the hand-feeder to the more limited attention available in the new home. If the bird is accustomed to spending the day out, it should begin spending a little more time in its cage while it is still with the hand-feeder.

When taking the youngster home, the juvenile grey's sense of security may be shaken. Take extra time helping the bird to feel comfortable in the new home. Each bird's adjustment time will vary. The young bird should not be left to fend for itself, physically or emotionally, right away. The human flock can reduce the amount of attention being provided as the bird becomes more comfortable.

through the compassionate encouragement of the social unit (caregivers).

When a young grey meets a new situation, it looks for cues as to how it should feel about that situation. If trusted humans are happy or excited, a grey will then usually not be afraid. The best way to instill the curiosity and confidence that are necessary for independence is for you as the caregiver to model them. You should also provide the young bird a safe haven from which to observe its surroundings when its confidence is shaky.

The newly weaned juvenile grey needs plenty of reassurance. It needs to know that it can get the attention of its owners when it needs to and that it is a welcome member of this new flock. It is not unusual for a juvenile grey to revert to making baby noises to announce its needs. A new bird owner might be afraid of "spoiling" the baby by responding to the cries, but, much like any other kind of baby, juvenile greys cry when they need something, and ignoring a crying baby can foster feelings of insecurity. The crying normally stops once the young bird feels secure.

As the baby's confidence grows, so will its curiosity. It depends on those around it to encourage development of an inquisitive nature. Unlike other parrots that will turn everything within reach into a toy, greys have to be taught to be this adventurous. Demonstrate toy play and shredding in front of the bird, showing excitement and delight

vocally. While playing with a toy, periodically present it to the bird briefly, then take it back and play some more. This type of modeling is even more effective if there's another parrot, person, or pet to join in. When the second party begins playing with the toy, you can gush praises. The baby bird will then want to join in the flock's games. This same game can be played with new foods or any other new accessory.

Vocal games also help promote independence. When the baby is practicing vocalizations, repeat some of the pleasant sounds back to the bird. The baby will stop to listen, but at the same time it will be encouraged to experiment more with this means of getting attention. Again, these interactive games encourage

Eating

Watch the newly weaned juvenile carefully to determine whether or not it's eating. Occasionally, a newly weaned grey parrot might stop eating and beg incessantly as a reaction to the stress of moving. Breeders mention this in their instructions to new owners and suggest bringing the bird back for a few days for resocialization. Many breeders with closed aviaries won't allow the bird's return, but will suggest telephone support and will be happy to offer reassurance and answer questions about whether the bird's failure to eat is physical or behavioral.

self-confidence, which help the young parrot gain independence.

Many juvenile greys do not want to eat when left alone with food. An older grey with more confidence will be less inhibited, but a juvenile bird will often prefer to wait until the more social activity of group feeding takes place. The bird might wait until someone is around to point out the food and to model eating it before it will even seem to notice that there is food in the bowl.

Greys that have not been taught independence are much more likely to develop phobic behaviors and problems such as feather disorders. With guidance, even older birds can learn independence and will be better off if they do. Independent birds and their owners better enjoy the time they spend together because both humans and bird are calmer and more predictable.

Begging Behaviors

Learned, regressed, or retained begging behaviors are occasionally seen in grey parrots. Crying and begging postures might indicate that the bird wasn't fully weaned, they might indicate that the bird regressed to an unweaned state, or they might mean something else entirely.

Our first concern is physical health. A newly weaned juvenile parrot is a fragile creature and can quickly succumb to illness. (A sudden physical decline, which might take only hours, is called "crashing.") If a fully weaned bird suddenly stops eating, it could be demonstrating a physical response to illness. If the weaned juvenile has not already been seen by an avian veterinarian by the time the crying problem appears, it should be taken to one as quickly as possible.

Occasionally, a young bird might be eating sufficiently when humans aren't there. Evaluate this possibility by weighing the bird the first thing every morning. An electronic scale that measures weight in grams is invaluable for this process. Keep a chart. If a healthy juvenile bird is losing weight, then we can presume that it is not getting sufficient nutrition. If the bird is being offered a healthy balanced diet, we must also presume that this bird is not eating independently.

Bird and caretaker will shape each other's behavior.

Begging behaviors can often be remedied with warm food immediately, first thing after weighing every morning. Offer warm baby formula, oatmeal, nutritious whole grain toast, or chunky food such as cooked pasta or sweet potatoes every morning before the begging starts. If you can get the food into the bird before the behavior begins, the behavior often will disappear immediately.

If the hand-feeder was using a dependable, balanced formula, offer that. Otherwise, try to find Harrison's Bird Diet (available through a veterinarian) or another balanced avian formula. Moisten the cubes and offer them wet and warm, 100 to 105°F (37.8 to 40.6°C), one at a time, from the hand. When offering fresh or thawed frozen mixed vegetables, try sprinkling the warm, moist mixture with a little Harrison's Juvenile Hand-feeding Formula. The hand-feeding formula increases protein and other important nutrients missing in the vegetables, and the wet mixture served warm probably resembles chunky premasticated (chewed) food from the parents.

Note: *Do not heat any parrot's food in a microwave oven.* Undetected hot spots develop that can burn the bird. Even professional hand-feeders are best advised not to use microwave ovens for the heating of parrot food.

Any parrot, but especially a young bird, will more willingly accept warm food than food at room temperature or cold. Jean Pattison suggests that giving a bird only a few bites of warm food from the hand can stimulate the bird to be interested in food in the bowl. Some birds will also want or may prefer a warm meal before bedtime.

Progressive Cooperation Techniques

Mother parrots snuggle, cuddle, and feed their babies when they are small, but once the babies are expected to learn to eat independently, their mother tries to redirect them to independent eating or other behaviors when they beg. Maturing neonates and juveniles turn to peers for allopreening and snuggling. Normal companion parrot babies also learn many other behaviors such as playing with toys, shredding toys, flapping, peek-a-boo, and vocal games. If they go to a new home during the developmental stage in which they are looking for peers to preen and to play with, they won't be as likely to fall back into begging behaviors.

1. Provide active constructive attention to a begging bird so that it learns more appropriate behavior.

2. Demonstrate independent eating by eating and offering to share food.

3. Initiate allopreening by gently scratching the jawbone, lores, ears, and nape.

4. Play with the bird with food toys when it's hungry.

5. Save those cuddles for evenings and naptimes and for occasional reassurance when confronted with unfamiliar (scary) things.

Juvenile grey parrots know they don't know what's best for them. They sit around flapping and looking expectant and waiting for someone to show them what to do. If the only coaching they have is how to cuddle, then cuddling is the only thing they will learn. In order to help the bird develop independent behaviors, including independent eating, owners should involve the baby in playing with toys, vocal "duets," climbing, exercising, shredding, and showering.

If the caretaker does not shape the bird's behavior, the bird will begin shaping the caregiver's behavior. This is generally not to the parrot's benefit. Independence and confidence are much easier to instill if behavioral training is begun within a few weeks of the bird's arrival.

Along with hope and anticipation, new owners often feel nervous, or maybe a little scared. They have just found the parrot of their dreams, and they don't want to do anything that might ruin its personality. However, with sensitive basic training and plenty of patience, both parrot and owner should enjoy a long life in each other's company.

During the first days or weeks in the new home, humans can easily reinforce acceptable behavior and establish a sense of security. A well-planned environment in which everyone consistently interacts with the bird and reinforces the bird's best responses, will enable the grey parrot's personality to blossom and allow the bird to explore different relationships with the members of its new flock. A juvenile grey will feel more secure knowing that its new keepers are predictable and trustworthy. Step-up practice and using labels or cues can establish predictability in the environment. Hands-on interactions such as the towel game can make the young parrot feel safe.

A bright-eyed young grey, brimming over with curiosity, will want to explore new things to the point of being almost afraid; then it will want to hide its head in a safe spot until it is sure there is nothing to be afraid of and curiosity kicks in again. Baby greys naturally feel safe in corners and small dark areas with other warm bodies close by. To help reinforce curiosity and security, this is the perfect time to introduce the towel game.

The Towel Game

A neonate or recently weaned juvenile can be carried around nestled in the loose folds of a towel as one might carry a baby or a doll. The young bird will enjoy familiar or unfamiliar surroundings from this ultra-safe vantage point. When it's fun for the bird, the towel becomes a very useful tool for several aspects of parrot ownership. The interaction is similar to playing peek-a-boo under the covers. (Cavity breeders spend a great deal of time in small places peeking out.)

Begin with a large towel or small blanket draped over your lap with the long ends hanging down on each side. Both size and color can be important. A too-small towel or a brightly colored or striped towel might not offer an appropriate sense of safety for some birds and many birds are afraid of the stripes. The most dependable early results will probably come from a gray towel the same color as the bird. Avoid knitted or crocheted afghans as their loose threads can easily entrap little toes and cause panic. Also, examine the towel first and trim away any loose threads.

Put the bird on your lap and put one hand under each end of the towel. Lift the ends up to a point where the bird feels comfortable with it. Some greys obviously prefer the ends high, making a sort of canyon or cavern inside the towel; others prefer the hands lower.

Eventually, sometimes right away, you can simply drape a towel over the bird and start playing "peek-a-bird." Most young greys will be calm and receptive to cuddling, head scratching, and feet rubbing during these interactions. Soon you should be able to cover only the bird's head with the towel and it will allow petting any place known to be enjoyable. (Favorite places include the neck, nostrils, top of the head, around the eyes, the wing pit, and the hollow under the mandible.)

There is no wrong way to play the towel game *if the bird enjoys the process.* A bird might be enticed to

Playing peek-a-boo in a towel furthers cooperation between bird and caretaker.

play when it sees you playing with another person or pet first. Greys are always tempted to join in when they see a "rival" having fun and getting attention. Take turns lifting up corners and "hiding" under the towel. Cover small pieces of a favorite food with a layer of towel. Whoever uncovers it first gets to eat it.

Throughout its lifetime, a parrot must submit to being restrained in a towel for veterinary examination or for grooming. Sometimes early reactions to too-aggressive or ill-planned toweling techniques can damage the bird's disposition. Early conditioning to enjoy the towel game will enable the young parrot to happily allow towel restraint. With good technique, even older greys can respond well to the towel game. By making the bird aware of the safety provided by a towel and by keeping a towel handy, a sense of safety can be provided any time and any place.

Grey parrots are very capable of forming relationships with different people in different ways. Consistent handling and cooperation practice establish a basis for trusting everyone. This is a matter of people-training here, as allowing untrained humans to handle a sensitive young bird in unfriendly or provocative ways can generate biting and fearfulness.

The goal of patterning exercises is not to maintain dominant status with a grey; step-ups and other cued interactions are cooperation exercises intended to build and maintain trust. Early step-ups are best practiced in unfrequented territory, away from the cage, for a minute or so a couple of times daily, and ended after a successful interaction.

Note: Do not encourage or allow anyone to wave fingers in the bird's face or to provoke the bird by poking at it with inanimate objects. Nothing could be worse for the bird's disposition. If the bird is resisting patterning by a less-favored person, then the favorite person can participate more fully in step-up practice. This practice must be discontinued if it stimulates either aggression or fearfulness; don't do anything that causes the bird either to bite or to be afraid.

Once a bird enjoys and cooperates with step-ups away from the cage, it can be stepped up from the cage top or door. Because of their shy nature, greys benefit from knowing that they are totally safe and in charge when in their cages. Rather than expecting the bird to step up inside the cage, let it choose whether to come out or not. Offer food and encouragement, but don't forcibly remove a young grey parrot; it may have a perfectly good reason to want to stay in the cage at that time. This behavior passes, usually within two or three weeks. If the bird establishes a pattern of not coming out at all, seek professional behavioral assistance.

Other Processes

From the bird's first days in the home, encourage it to remain open and accepting of relationships with several individuals. This should be rather easy, for, as we have previously observed, well-socialized juvenile greys are usually ready, willing, and able to form relationships with different people. If the bird is reluctant to interact with multiple individuals, the favorite person might pattern with out-of-territory interactions such as step-ups, rescues, and outings. However, interactions should not be forced. It's not unusual for a young bird to feel the need to solidify a predictable relationship with the most favored person before exploring relationships with others. A new human/bird bond can be facilitated with transportation—taking the time to move the bird from one bird-approved place to another.

A grey parrot of any age is more likely to stay tame if it is handled daily. Love, cuddling, and playing the towel game at least once each week will pattern the bird to intimate and restrictive handling. Many, but not all, companion greys like to be petted on the neck as do many other parrots, but most baby greys like to be hugged or snuggled.

Remember to facilitate and reinforce curiosity. Encourage the bird to play independently by your side rather than demanding face-to-face interactions with humans every moment. Carefully reinforce appropriate intellectual exploration, as a grey may become protective of certain items, such as a food dish, a favorite toy, or a chrome appliance. If a grey is protecting an area or object, step the bird up onto a hand-held perch or allow it to leave the protected area before picking it up.

To avoid frightening the bird, maintain eye contact with your nose pointed to the side and only one eye visible to the bird. A baby grey that knows you're watching is less likely to act up; it may give little pinches to regain your attention.

Establishing Cues: The Power of Suggestion

During the "honeymoon" period, it is especially easy to teach a juvenile grey the meaning of the words "Good bird." Use these words generously. Birds also love to hear "Pretty bird" and "I love you." They especially enjoy these phrases when spoken with enthusiasm. Demonstrating vocal affection provides a valuable precedent for maintaining good behaviors in the future.

If the bird knows that good things come to good birds, we can use these positive words as cues to suggest appropriate behavior. This is more effective than the use of "No" or "Don't" or "Stop," which might temporarily interrupt a bird but won't necessarily prevent the behavior by selecting an alternative. If we say, instead, "Be a good bird," we remind the bird of those good things that come to good birds, and we are more likely to have guided the bird to appropriate behavior, not merely caused hesitation. This can be a tremendously powerful tool during the coming developmental period and beyond.

A bird can be taught to discontinue a particular behavior by using a stern, straight-on gaze and the cue, "Be careful." The setup goes like this: When the juvenile bird is about to experience something you know it will dislike—whether that's falling off a swing or a chewed perch or losing its grip on a hand—say to the bird "Be careful." The bird learns to associate the words "Be careful" with something unwanted occurring. Practice giving the bird a stern look with eyes wide open in order to convey a sense of limits. However, straight-on eye contact may be too threatening for a shy or phobic juvenile grey, as it resembles the stalking gaze of a predator. With a very shy young grey, even a stern look might have to be delivered with only one eye.

In the future you can simply say "*Be careful*" when you want to redirect behavior. The interruption provided may be brief. Sometimes, reminding the bird to be a good bird is enough to stimulate different behavior, but other times, you may have to go over and move the bird in order to physically prevent potentially dangerous or destructive activities.

Transitional Nipping

During these precious early days in the home, nips should be rare and experimental. The best way to deal with occasional nips and pinches is to avoid situations where they occur and to simply ignore them. Remember that most behaviors that are not reinforced probably disappear.

Don't take it personally when a juvenile grey experiments on flesh with its beak. The young parrot must be handled in ways in which nipping is not possible so that these behaviors cannot be repeatedly enacted and inadvertently reinforced into patterns. This means not putting fingers in front of the beak. When stepping up, announce the interaction, then move your hand toward the feet from below. When petting the neck, hold the bird close so it has the opportunity to press its face into the security of a shirt while the hand approaches. A grey might love being scratched, but an approaching hand can be scary enough to provoke a nip.

Previously Owned and Wild-caught Greys

An adoption or resale grey parrot with good companion potential is probably a domestic bird that is no more than three to six years old. A grey parrot that has not been handled might be either aggressive or terrified (or sometimes both), but moving the bird will make a noticeable difference. Maladjusted greys often respond positively to being moved, and a new home often brings radically improved behavior almost spontaneously.

The last legal wild-caught grey parrots entered the United States in 1992. During the last decade of importation, many of these birds came in so calm and tame or close to tame that it was easy to suspect that they were being captive-bred rather than captured. In many cases, the only way to identify a resocialized wild-caught grey from a resocialized hand-fed is by the open band. Many of these birds make fine companions. If these wild-caught greys live to their 50s or 60s, they will remain occasionally available in the United States through the middle of this century.

Although older and possibly never before socialized to human touch, for a person with great patience, these birds can offer good companion potential. These birds require the same veterinary examination and quarantine as other birds. They may experience stages of behavioral development similar to those of a domestic baby parrot as they acclimate to the new home. Similar behavioral strategies and socialization processes as with hand-feds are used, but changes must be made more slowly, with this exception: A new hand-fed grey parrot baby should be held for limited periods only, guiding it to learn to play alone (develop independence). An older, bird-bonded or wild-caught grey parrot can be held for long periods of time to build and improve the human/grey bond if the bird is enjoying the interaction.

Not every parrot makes a good companion. Just as some birds prefer to live with humans, others prefer to live with birds. A parrot may be so entrenched in its wild roles, so intent on its own personal motivations, that it is completely unable to live with humans. Every moment in the company of humans can represent life-threatening stress to such a bird. Every effort should be made to provide the bird with as natural an environment as possible, with an attempt being made to shield this bird from contact with humans.

Adjustment and Rehabilitation

Most grey parrots are cautious, and changing homes can be unsettling. Every effort should be made to help the bird feel safe. It's probably a good idea to leave a towel or blanket, being careful of strings that might trap little toenails, over at least

Leg bands are the most common form of traceable identification.

half the cage for the first few days. Try setting the cage at chest level first, and if the bird seems nervous, try either raising or lowering the cage until the bird seems more at ease. If there are no other established birds in the living area, situate the new grey in the living area, but well out of traffic areas.

The changes encountered when coming to a new home usually provide a temporary window of opportunity for reinforcing good behavior. This is similar to the "honeymoon period" experienced by baby hand-feds coming into the first home, but the window of good behavior may be very brief. Work quickly and consistently to make the most of this fleeting opportunity.

An adoption grey may have had little or no interaction with humans in a long time and may not have received the best care, so begin rehabilitation by taking the bird immediately to an avian veterinarian, possibly even before taking the bird home. Observe appropriate quarantine procedures as specified by the veterinarian, especially if there are other birds in the home. This period will probably be at least one to three months, during which time the new parrot must be behaviorally rehabilitated. If behavioral rehabilitation is not begun until after quarantine, you may have already missed the window of opportunity to easily reinforce appropriate behavior. Ask the veterinarian to examine and update the bird's wing feather trim. This is important in training or retraining the bird to step ups.

Understanding Time

Even before attempting to handle the new bird, the environment can be planned to assist its behavioral adjustment. A bird inhabiting a controlled environment never sees the shadows grow long, then short, then long, or hears the frogs start croaking exactly 30 minutes before sundown. An indoor bird never knows the heat of the noonday sun followed by cooling afternoon showers. These are all natural cycles that enable a wild bird to easily perceive the passage of time.

Include environmental elements that demonstrate the passage of time—a singing bird clock, a full-spectrum light that comes on and goes off every day at the same time,

or a television that is set to come on at the same time with the same program every day for regular TV time. These time markers in the indoor environment are helpful in conditioning a grey parrot to tolerate being left alone during the day. That is, if the bird is accustomed to having an in-home companion all day, and that companion then goes to work outside the home, the bird might develop adverse behavioral reactions related to feeling abandoned. If TV time is well established before any radical schedule changes are made, the bird will not usually react negatively to other changes. TV time will be a constant in an ever-changing world. The presence of these types of constants also helps to acclimate the bird to accept change.

Direct Interaction

Begin interactions with a wary bird by playing eye games and approaching with nonthreatening posture. It is best to establish contact with the bird first with games involving no eye contact and progress to games involving limited eye contact.

If the bird can be handled and is not too frightened, hold it as much as possible during the first 48 hours in the new home. If it can be accomplished productively, work on step-up patterning for as long as you and the bird seem to enjoy doing it. Try to be nurturing, supportive, and consistent. Handle the bird less if it seems to tire easily, perhaps providing a little extra heat and sleep time for the first few days.

Even though the relocated bird should have no strongly developed instincts to defend new territory, be sure to practice step-ups in a contained area outside the bird's new home territory. Be sure also to pattern the bird to step up onto a hand-held perch as well as onto hands. The bird may be reluctant to step up from the cage, so don't attempt step-ups from the cage unless the bird is first well patterned to step-ups in unfamiliar territory.

A young resale domestic bird should be socialized exactly as a baby grey would. A two-to-three-year-old grey in a new home should go through a "honeymoon period" similar to the baby days, followed by the "terrible twos" just as a baby bird would, but these developmental phases will be of much shorter duration with the older bird.

Dietary Improvements

When the bird's diagnostic tests come back, ask the veterinarian before trying to improve the bird's diet by supplementing vitamins. If the bird has a less-than-healthy liver or kidneys, be very careful about vitamin supplementation, especially with D_3, which could kill the bird. Better to improve diet with real food: Fresh fruits, vegetables, pasta, and a quality commercial diet (see Changing a Grey Parrot's Diet, page 71). Almost any food—quality whole grain toast, macaroni and cheese, or oatmeal—served warm should seem like love to a previously hand-fed grey that has been neglected. A grey

A mature grey may view unfamiliar foods cautiously.

parrot that is responding to the love inspired by warm food will probably want to feed you.

A newly adopted grey parrot may prefer to eat nothing but seeds, especially sunflower or safflower seeds. This is similar to adopting a child who will eat only French fries. Put these birds on a canary-based mix as quickly as possible, then you can begin familiarizing the bird with a pelleted diet. Eventually wean the bird to the pelleted diet.

Chapter Three
Developing Behavior

From weaning to the onset of sexual maturity, a juvenile grey carefully studies everything it sees and touches. In the wild these feathered students would be following adult flock members around, mimicking their actions: grooming as they groom, eating what they eat, communicating as they communicate. What is learned during this developmental period, along with inherited traits, combine to form the individual's personality. Curiosity buds, then blooms. The grey parrot is developing confidence needed for a successful life—picking up cues from its environment and developing relationships with its companions, feathered or unfeathered. It's establishing a social identity—status—a comfortable position—in the flock.

While younger greys might seek attention from anyone, maturing juveniles become more selective about who holds, and therefore, controls them. In nature, flocks with the strongest members live longer and have more babies. Young parrots survive by studying more established and successful members of the flock—more confident individuals—and copying their behavior.

These "teachers" have proved their prowess by surviving and reproducing. Young birds also watch weaker members and distance themselves from individuals that might jeopardize the well-being of the flock.

Indoors or out, a juvenile grey will place more trust in individuals it perceives to be stronger or more fit. The bird might judge a person by the self-confidence projected or by an event in which the person proved to be worthy or unworthy. During the developmental period, a juvenile grey is likely to test the person in order to form a judgment. Of course, this test often involves use of the beak. Judgments it makes or grudges it develops during this stage may last a very long time.

Passing Phases

Nipping: Grey owners often report that their birds go through a nippy stage or stages during the first years in the home. This experimental nipping is normal behavioral development as a well-adjusted grey begins showing signs of the strength of personality and independence necessary to be an adult. If the bird has been carefully guided to develop confidence, the grey in this phase might be a contrary and determined creature similar to a human child in the "terrible twos." The youngster becomes increasingly exploratory and experimental. This behavioral phase is both expected and beneficial. It should appear, at least momentarily, or there may be concern that the bird will not develop confidence.

Shyness: Many grey owners also report that their birds go through a shy stage during this same period. In some birds, the nippy stage might be prominent; in some birds, the shy stage will be prominent. Either or both stages might appear suddenly but both stages might be virtually unnoticeable in a bird that is handled frequently and socialized as suggested in this book. Shyness can also disappear suddenly. A young grey parrot is probably stimulated to overcome shyness when it meets a potential mate. If a shy young grey has a "thunderbolt"—an immediate "matelike" attraction to a particular human—that impulse can be exploited, stimulated, and reinforced, and almost immediately, the bird can become less shy with everyone.

Fight-or-flight: During the developmental period the bird might exhibit dramatic instinctual reactions to perceived danger. This fight-or-flight response is part of the bird's necessary survival mechanism in the wild. If a juvenile companion grey was not previously well patterned, it

Avoiding Preditors

A big part of a wild bird's survival mechanism involves not being eaten. This takes endless, relentless watchfulness, the ability to accurately identify danger, and quick reactions. If the young grey comes to view humans as predators because of a frightening incident, it can't help but try to avoid humans. If a human picks up a grey while it is panicking, the bird might associate that person with being afraid, possibly viewing that person in the same light that it might view a predator. The parrot might then bite that person out of fear. Fear bites are much harder than bites intended to cause fear.

risks losing confidence in the bond with humans. If patterned behavioral controls—step ups, the towel game, assisting with transportation—are not habitual, changes can appear swiftly.

A fight-or-flight response is significantly more intense than simply ducking into a corner. Once it appears, we must be careful not to frustrate or reinforce resulting behavior. Our experience suggests that the earlier a strong enactment of the fight-or-flight response (panic) appears, the more likely it is to be enduring. The enactment of a fight-or-flight response by a mature grey will probably be of more temporary duration than fearfulness developing in a grey under one year of age.

Budding Confidence

A typical new parrot owner wants to provide the bird with everything it needs. To achieve this, the new owner might buy the best food, a fantastic cage, lots of toys, and shower the bird with attention. However, as a wild animal, the African grey has evolved the intelligence, strength, and determination to meet its own needs. As to humans, the parrot experiences stress when it doesn't feel able to do this or feels that it has little control over its life.

While other parrots are naturally inclined to take control and are independent by nature, the grey has to learn to realize this potential. During the developmental period, the young bird is an intellectual sponge. It craves learning how to explore, interact, and function on its own, and how to fit into the social group.

Play and exploration are easily facilitated at this age. The bird benefits from having a safe haven—a vantage point—to return to when feeling overwhelmed, either under a towel or blanket, in the crook of the arm, or in the lap. The bird can then be presented with opportunities to investigate. Both the person and the bird can get down on a blanket on the floor to play with a variety of toys together. The owner can demonstrate shredding and jangling while the baby watches to see if anything bad happens or if its role model is having fun. They can travel to new rooms in the house together and meet new people. Studying these activities at

Freedom of Choice

Avoid the formation of phobias or fearfulness by providing opportunities to make successful decisions. In an inadequately designed environment, a young parrot can easily get into trouble, and we might wind up constantly retrieving the bird from destructive or dangerous experiences. Any impediment to budding curiosity can damage the youngster's personality.

Like humans who are bound by culture, convention, commitment, and yes, by danger, the closest thing a companion parrot has to "freedom" is the opportunity to decide how and where to spend time. Even if a bird chooses not to play on a particular perch or not to play with a particular toy, the presence of that second toy or perch has provided an opportunity for the bird to experience success. The process enhances confidence, self-worth, and a sense of comfort.

this age allows the bird to entertain itself in the absence of flock members and allows it to keep its composure when scenery changes.

Feelings of involvement can be fostered by including the bird in what ordinarily would be flock activities. Responding to pleasant vocalizations encourages responses and provides the bird with a chance to learn to ask for the things it needs. The bird will want to be included in mealtimes. It will need to be able to see when flock members are coming or going, and will want to participate in group activities even if that is watching television.

Testing and Potential Setbacks

Anyone wishing to handle a grey parrot must earn the bird's trust while keeping his or her skin intact. The first step is to maintain "grey-friendly" posture. A bird that feels threatened or defensive bites harder. Body language that can be interpreted as friendly to a grey includes moving the head forward and lower than usual. Squinting eyes slightly and looking sideways at the bird will also be interpreted as friendly. Making a long, low, "*Hellooooo*" sound or a clucking or knocking noise with the tongue also helps establish cordial interaction. These gestures may be included in routine cooperation exercises and the daily time out of the cage. Every time you respond to the grey in a friendly and predictable manner, you are building trust.

When approaching for stepping up, announce your intentions before offering your hand to the bird. Saying "*Step up*" first and then again as you place your hand near the bird's feet allows it to adjust to what is going to happen. A grey is much more cooperative if it is not caught off guard, if it knows what is going to happen next. If the bird reaches for

Grey parrots enjoy having their feathers caressed and fluffed rather than stroked smooth.

your fingers with its beak, say nothing, but move your hand toward the bird's chest until it lets go, then continue moving your hand toward the bird's feet to complete step up.

Young birds may have difficulty containing their enthusiasm while being handled. Gestures that begin affectionately may become painful as the bird's excitement increases; therefore, it's best to simply stay out of the way of the beak. Affectionately restraining the head while petting can be effective in distracting the bird and can enable it to regain self-control. Ideally, provide an alternative object for the bird to chew. Especially, if the bird is focused on chewing its "perch" (the hand it's standing on), it may be provided with a small "holding" toy to chew instead.

not ready to take control of the social and behavioral environment and will not feel secure in that role. Its reaction might be to bite harder the next time you approach, and subsequent bites will have much more behind them than earlier tests. This display of insecurity, sometimes to the point of fear, is an exercise in frustration.

Fear Response

An older bird might seize any opportunity to take control of the situation and accept that this "weak" human should be aggressively pushed away from the "strong" flock. For a young grey, a fear response may be part of this response. If you continue to back down from the bird, it may actually become afraid to associate with you. Because fearful greys have a much harder bite, these frightened birds might wind up being labeled as "mean" or even "vicious." The more often you try unsuccessfully to handle a frightened bird, the more afraid the bird will become.

To break this cycle, immediately stop trying to handle the bird. Repeatedly forcing unsuccessful interaction can cause a grey parrot to hold one of the grudges these birds are notorious for. Whenever moving forward fails, it's time to move back to successful interactions, sometimes back to the beginning of the relationship. If the bird has been spooked enough to not want to come out of the cage, then you must use friendly postures and

If your skin becomes too closely involved with the inside of a bird's beak, the bird is testing to decide how to view you. Pulling away and yelling *"Ouch! Bad bird!"* is a clear message that you are not guiding the relationship. This can be uncomfortable for a grey in the developmental period. A bird at this age is

Manipulating the Perception of Territory

If a grey increasingly exhibits territorial-related aggression, try rearranging and moving the cage and play areas. Occasional outings where the bird is handled by sensitive, astute strangers can be used to manipulate excessive bonding and territorial tendencies and improve cooperation. Don't forget the importance of a separate roost/cage and foraging territories such as a play area or second cage, and the role of moving from one place to another—carrying the bird—encourages, supports, and maintains cooperative behavior.

Of course, one bird might need more careful patterning, while another needs more stimulation, and still another bird might absolutely *have* to have a bath every day. Anticipate the bird's physical and emotional needs as a means of preventing unwanted experimentation with spontaneous innovated—sometimes unexpected—activities. Negative behaviors appearing during the developmental period can become habitual and long lasting.

talk to the bird through the bars. The bird can begin to get used to your hands being in sight or resting on the cage. It must get used to the cage door being open. Patiently allow the bird to choose when it wants to come out of the cage.

It's not unusual for a caregiver to shower affection and concern on a parrot that is acting afraid. If this happens a few times, the bird might then decide that the best way to get affection is to act afraid. The owner is generally better off letting the bird calm down alone and then providing attention and reassurance when the bird has regained composure. The towel game can also be used to reinforce security in a bird that is conditioned to the game.

If the bird is reacting fearfully, you can regain the parrot's respect with the help of another person. This person should be someone either the bird already trusts or someone who can easily win the bird's trust. This person can "reintroduce" you.

Testing Limits

A juvenile parrot tests the limits of acceptable behavior by challenging the status and authority of "flock members" in other ways. Annoying vocalizations, roaming, chasing, and any other unacceptable behaviors must be addressed before they become a permanent part of the bird's personality. They are best eliminated by being made inaccessible, not being reinforced, and by providing alternative activities.

Successful cooperation patterning means frequent handling with no bites. Ineffective handling can sometimes be worse than no handling, but no handling is also bad during this period. If the bird is beginning to bite repeatedly during this period, use the towel game, interactive submissive postures, hand-held perches, or stop handling the bird, play eye games, and seek professional assistance right away.

Growing Feathers and Related Responses

Greys begin molting wing feathers at around 12 months old. Often, the first flight feathers to molt out are primaries near the end of the wing. Once immature primary flight feathers—blood feathers—reach a certain length they are fragile and sensitive. If the young bird's wing feathers have been trimmed, especially if those feathers were trimmed very short, the blood feather will have little protection and can break simply through the act of flap.

Young greys between 12 and 18 months might suddenly decide to avoid any activities involving flapping the wings if undeveloped feathers are in danger of breaking. This may mean that a bird might avoid coming out of the cage for two to three weeks while new (blood) feathers finish developing. If you insist that the bird come out of the cage during this time, the bird might become very nervous when you approach, although it may still tolerate handling by others. Just let the bird finish growing wing feathers, then, if handling problems remain, they can be addressed when the parrot is out of danger of being

The "Fickle" Grey Parrot

Greys usually switch loyalties toward the end of the developmental period. The grey has changing needs to be met from a favored companion and is trying to meet those needs. A young grey wants to associate with someone strong. Toward the end of the developmental period, the bird may switch loyalties to someone it sees more as an equal. A grey parrot will probably not want a mate that will boss it around, nor does it want a mate that cannot stand up for itself.

To solidify a new mate-type relationship, the grey may feel compelled to push the former favorite person away. This is usually temporary. If the former favorite person can wait it out, he or she will regain acceptance, as long as that person hasn't lost the bird's trust. Patience is the key. Grey parrots are very social by nature and like to have many companions. They usually form relationships with everyone in the family when given a chance.

physically (and, as a result, emotionally) damaged.

As Time Goes By

The young grey parrot might become so cooperative that we are tempted to discontinue step-up practice and the towel game. This is not a good idea even if the bird seems totally docile at this time.

Usually, however, at least one nippy period will come and go between the developmental period and the appearance of sexually related behaviors that might be called adolescence.

The techniques described here are intended to enhance favorable behaviors in companion greys and to suppress or minimize most behaviors related to breeding. Some greys will be kept easily tame; some will be difficult. Expect every bird to be a little different, with vast differences between successfully socialized birds and unsocialized birds. If all interactions are consistent, the bird will be more predictable.

As breeding age approaches, expect heightened exploration, and physical and emotional experimentation. The bird might change emotional and/or territorial loyalties, becoming aggressive around a newly selected territory or a new favorite human (mate substitute). It might be necessary to take an arrogant young grey out of familiar territory for at least a few days each year in order to repattern the bird to cooperate and interact with unfamiliar humans. Vacations and indoor "outings" (visits to unfamiliar territory) are helpful at this time. Even a simple car ride with the bird in a carrier can make a wonderful difference in a parrot's disposition. Careful transporting and meticulous wing

feather trims will ensure safety on these outings.

Sexual Maturity, Fearfulness, and Aggression

A maturing grey parrot might become increasingly concerned with immediate environmental control. The bird might begin attacking tissues or people sneezing or blowing into tissues. It might also attack someone cleaning with quick motions using paper towels. A maturing grey might suddenly decide it loves, or hates, a particular dog or cat, or stuffed animal.

If allowed a great deal of liberty in the home, the bird might become

Wooden furniture may be viewed and chewed like a toy rather than a piece of furniture to be simply admired.

hypervigilant or aggressive around a suddenly and mysteriously selected territory. Beware the presence of mirrors, chrome, and glass. A maturing grey will be seeking both companions and rivals in their reflections.

Toys

Provide at least one "enemy" (preferably a toy) to be regularly thwarted. To a very real extent, the bird must select or identify this enemy independently. Of course, it's very important for this enemy to not

be a living creature or a treasured human possession, so several potential, approved surrogate enemies must be provided. Safe, unbreakable toys and loud, bird-safe bells are excellent candidates. If a young companion grey has no opportunity to express natural territorial impulses, it is likely to begin expressing that natural parrot energy against anyone or anything close.

If the bird is enjoying attacking a toy, leave them alone. The parrot is unlikely to be cooperative at this time. There will continue to be many times when the bird will solicit human attention. It's best to handle a grey parrot when the experience is more likely to be successful. The more successful behavioral experiences you have at this time, and the more the bird is patterned and reinforced to cooperate, the more likely the bird is to cooperate when it becomes fully mature.

Confidence

As grey parrots mature, they may become increasingly obsessed with control of their immediate environment. If they feel they have no control, or if they are repeatedly pushed in ways that stimulate and reinforce panic, they will become increasingly shy. If you see a trend of developing fearfulness, take steps to improve the bird's confidence, perhaps allowing it to live higher or lower, depending upon the bird, allowing it to occasionally choose whether to leave the cage on its own or maybe simply hide. The addition of a small tent open on two sides might be an excellent choice for a shy grey. It's not unusual to see a temporary increase in aggressive behaviors as fearful phases subside. This isn't where we want to wind up, but it's part of the process of leaving fear behind. It's what we want to see at this time.

Aggression

Eventually, threats may be accompanied by aggression; a bite actually breaks the skin. During this

Chewing and Other Signs of Romance

By three years of age, a normal grey parrot will begin exhibiting some pretty impressive chewing behaviors. This is when the bird is starting to say to the world: "See what a good parent I could be!" As chewing behaviors develop, be sure to increase the number and frequency of fresh chewables in the cage or the play area.

As with human children, new behaviors will seem to appear suddenly out of nowhere. For months, the bird may ignore the picture frame behind the cage, then one day, all that remains is a pile of splinters on the floor. For years, the bird might put nothing into its water, then one day it might begin filling the water bowl with debris. A maturing grey parrot might suddenly begin pulling newspaper up through the bottom grate.

All of these behaviors are part of the grey parrot's instinctive need to attract a suitable mate. An industrious mate is probably highly prized in the wild. We can't punish a bird for chewing up things when it's doing its darndest to be the best that it can be. We must provide appropriate things to chew and reward the bird for chewing appropriately.

"Good Hand/Bad Hand"

A bird might begin to bite even a well-placed hand prompt for the step-up command. The most common time for a nip or bite of a hand offered for step-ups is when the bird is being removed from a familiar perch, the inside of the cage, or the top of the cage. This behavior can usually be defeated with improved technique and more frequent step-up practice in unfamiliar territory.

Maintain eye contact and offer the hand to be stepped on, approaching from below, as usual. Just as the prompt hand begins its approach to the bird, present an unfamiliar object just out of reach of the bird's beak (with one hand) and give the "step-up" command (with the other hand) followed by *"Be a good bird."*

That is, if a bird is threatening to bite the hand I want it to step on, I can pick up a small object (a spoon or a telephone or a piece of junk mail) and hold it about an inch below and in front of the bird's beak, give the step-up command, and suggest good behavior. Usually the surprised bird, responding to the familiar behavioral pattern, and knowing what "good bird" means, responds also by being what it is expected to be (a good bird).

Eye contact is especially important here. A bird will often maintain eye contact rather than bite. If the bird's eye is distracted by the introduced object, it will seek to regain eye contact immediately rather than take the time to bite after being distracted.

Even if the bird bites, that unfamiliar object (rather than the hand being offered) will probably be bitten. Care must be taken to ensure that the distraction device is not frightening to a shy parrot. The distraction object must be neither too large (which might scare the bird off the perch), too small (which might be ineffective), nor toxic (a lead or painted object).

time we may see both predictable and unpredictable bites especially in the bird's perceived territory. Usually there is plenty of warning: hypervigilance, eye movement, raised feathers across the shoulders or tops of wings, charging with beak open, or any other body language that usually accompanies aggression in this individual. If a grey parrot has not been appropriately socialized during the developmental period, attempts to resocialize the mature bird might be met with stubborn resistance.

The best way to deal with aggression appearing at the onset of sexual maturity—somewhere around five or six years—is to give the bird space to be obnoxious. That is not to say, reinforce obnoxious behavior. Never allow the grey parrot to chase or harass. Calmly remind the bird to

"*Be a good bird*," then return it to the cage. A bird nipping during a step-up might be sensitively wobbled by the hand it is sitting on. A bird being prompted to step up might be distracted with a toy or other inanimate object when being given the prompt for "*Step up.*" We call this distraction technique "Good Hand/Bad Hand."

You might also choose to handle an otherwise well-adapted bird either with the towel or with hand-held perches during nippy stages. You might even discontinue interactive behavior for a while if you suspect that the bird is going through a wing feather molt, breeding season, or some other difficult transitional period. Don't give the bird any opportunity to bite. Careful techniques can help to maintain tameness here, for if the bird has no chance to bite, biting can't be reinforced. Increasing access to "rainfall" (showers), destructible chewables, and exercise can help to compensate for pent-up energy that might otherwise be expressed as aggression.

Maturing greys occasionally decide that a particular chrome appliance is either a mate or a rival, leading to many courtships with toasters and wars with hair dryers. A grey parrot might decide that no one is allowed near the coffeepot. A bird that has fixated on a human-owned object must be denied access to that object. If it attacks a human-

owned object, pick the bird up using a hand-held perch, a towel, or the "Good Hand/Bad Hand" technique, and replace the object with an approved surrogate enemy toy. Again, we must encourage and reward a companion grey for expressing hostility against the approved enemy toy. Hostile energy will be expressed somehow; it is best expressed against a toy. The bird will continue to seek human interaction. As discussed, patterning for cooperation with step-ups, the towel game, and an ever-changing environment remain the most dependable ways to maintain companionability as the grey parrot matures.

Chapter Four

The Talking Grey Parrot

Not everyone who sees a grey parrot for the first time is attracted to its looks, and only later does an appreciation for its intelligence develop. The primary incentive that catapults grey parrots into so many human homes is its reputation for talking.

Like humans, greys are K-strategists, maturing slowly, who survive with learned rather than instinctual behavior. In the past, many companion grey parrots didn't acquire words until after one year of age. Today's premium hand-fed baby greys not only talk earlier, they are also speaking more openly in human settings. Even though greys have always enjoyed a reputation for acquiring, accurately reproducing, and using words, they were also known for being extremely quiet around strangers and in unfamiliar places.

The Quest

Male and female greys probably have equal ability to mimic, with both genders often acquiring large, constantly growing vocabularies. A more demonstrative, experimental, exuberant bird of either gender is more likely to want to communicate than a shy, withdrawn bird.

- Look for a bird that is interactive and interested in sights and sounds.
- Look for a baby that expresses interest and attention by leaning closer, stretching its wings—singly with a leg out or both shoulders stretched straight up—shaking the head while listening, or quickly wagging its tail from side to side. These easily observable happiness behaviors are indications that the bird is interested in what is going on around it.
- If the bird is old enough and has eyes that are light enough to see iris movement in contrast to the pupil of the eye, sometimes a grey will show interest by narrowing the pupils while keeping the eyelids almond-shaped. This is called "pinpointing" or "flashing."

A new owner may feel most confident about the bird's age, health, and socialization during hand-feeding by actually selecting a baby before it is weaned, and visiting frequently, usually once a week, to handle and interact with the bird. Speech training can begin before the bird is weaned, although, as we have repeatedly emphasized, grey parrots should be weaned by experienced professionals.

Talking, Mimicking, and Signaling

In the past, it was thought that one-on-one interaction, including much out-of-context repetition, was the best way to teach parrots to talk. If this worked at all, these birds were more likely to merely mimic the sounds of the words rather than to use the words with associated meaning. Modern parrot fanciers are more excited about the prospect of talking rather than mimicking parrots, so our ways have changed.

The work of Dr. Irene Pepperberg demonstrated that attempts to train grey parrots with audio- and video-tapes were useless. Her bird, Alex, developed his abilities to speak with understanding through use of the model/rival method, in which one bird interacts with two humans who demonstrate the behaviors (words and identification) that are being trained. One trainer questions the other human about colors, shapes, and objects. This person is both modeling behavior and functioning as a rival for the trainer's attention. The model answers the question and receives a reward. Sometimes, roles of model/rival and trainer are reversed.

This technique probably resembles the way young parrots learn to

communicate with their flock, by listening to older birds "duet" or talk back and forth. Although it is best to include humans or other talking birds in this process, if the bird is young and not too distracted, or if the bird is properly conditioned, the "rival" might even be one of those stuffed, talking parrot plush toys or the family dog. Parrots often pick up names quickly due to the obvious response they get.

In addition to the acquisition of language, grey parrots, especially,

acquire signaling behaviors. The most famous of the grey parrot's signals is probably that ear-splitting alarm call that is often used in captivity to demand attention. Grey parrots in the wild and in companion settings are fond of other types of signaling such as tapping the beak against the wall to mean: *"Are you there?" "Is this hollow?"* Or, they may make whistling or clicking sounds (happy recognition), or "gulping" interpretations of expressions of appreciation such as *"Oh, boy"* and *"Golly."*

Signals are less complex than actual language and may be more fun for birds. Some grey parrots enjoy signaling so much that they prefer signaling rather than using language. The most annoying signaling behaviors are often learned by companion greys for the purpose of getting immediate human attention. If a car alarm or smoke detector is annoying enough to make humans jump and to pay immediate frantic attention, then you can be sure that a young, gregarious grey parrot might learn to attract attention with that annoying signal after hearing it only once; in this case, the model/rival is the object making the noise.

Setting the Stage for Talking

A baby parrot needs a tremendously stimulating environment. For at least the first two years, the baby grey's environment should look a little like a nursery school, with lots of toys and interesting things lying around. Repetition is important, but you should speak to the baby parrot just as you would speak to an infant, expecting it to learn the words it hears most often. Use words in context, just as you would use them with a baby. The bird doesn't have to be held during speech training; much of a young parrot's first communication efforts will probably be used to induce you to pick it up.

Try a little "baby (parrot) talk,"— making the same sounds the young bird makes, for your first step to success might be in baby parrot language. If you can make a sound the bird is known to make, and the bird repeats the sound, it can then be rewarded with praise and affection, and you will have established the pattern by which the bird will acquire words. Grey parrots love to learn to use the expressions "Good bird!" and "Oh boy!" to signal happiness. Use soothing, cooing sounds if the bird is shy.

While a young grey will not usually be immediately able to repeat a word, early signs of progress include the bird sitting around "muttering" or "babbling" quietly. Expect to see pinpointing eyes at these times. The baby parrot will pick up the cadence of human language first, with understandable words and phrases following after practice.

Early phrases that are easily acquired include "What'cha doin'?" and anything with "itty" sounds such as "Pretty bird" and "Here, kitty, kitty, kitty." Once you start combining words into phrases, mix them up, like "Pretty kitty" and "What's kitty doin'?"

The most important part of teaching a grey parrot to talk is answering the bird. The more the flock responds, even to "baby bird talk," the more the young bird will practice.

While grey parrots can easily copy words from humans of either gender, it's not unusual for African greys to acquire deep "male" voices. The voice the bird mimics can tell us which human the bird is most bonded to, for greys, especially, tend to mimic the voice of the perceived human rival for the affections of their favorite person.

Singing quietly, almost directly, into the grey parrot's head is an excellent way to get its undivided attention. Grey parrots, even talking ones, don't pinpoint or flash their eyes as much as Amazons or *Poicephalus*, so the absence of obvious eye movement is not necessarily an indication that a grey won't talk.

Whistling Games and Daily Activities

Whistling games can be an exciting form of comunication for both

the bird and human flockmates. These games are probably virtually unavoidable with a grey parrot. Copying tunes from each other and adding onto the other's song is a source of entertainment, bonding, and either human or bird-initiated play. Use whistling as fun and words for labeling actions and objects; however, if you run over to the bird when it whistles instead of encouraging it to say "*Come here*" or "*Step up*," the bird will lose the motivation to learn these words.

Be sure to include the young parrot in daily activities: eating, sleeping, showering, and expressing affection to other humans and animals. These activities replicate the feeling of being part of the flock and should stimulate the baby parrot's natural instinct to communicate with other flock members. If there is no problem with aggression, some grey parrots benefit from being allowed to

sit higher than anybody else during speech training.

A baby grey will learn that the most exciting words it hears are useful words that are spoken with the most gusto and enthusiasm, or words that get the biggest reaction. Therefore, profanity and angry words might be learned with only one repetition if the bird is really "tuned in" to humans in the household.

Some grey parrots talk first for attention, so they might try to talk more when they can hear, but not see, humans. They talk first for attention in order to get out of the cage. This stimulus has been called "barrier frustration," for it has long been observed that caged birds or birds housed around a corner or screen appear to talk more than birds housed on open perches. This predisposition to vocalize in the presence of barriers is also a possible consequence of the feeling of safety provided by barriers. This doesn't mean that a grey will start talking if moved to another room. In some cases, you might want to spend time in another room to give the bird a chance to talk.

The Guaranteed Talking Parrot

Sometimes, even though you've done everything humanly possible to encourage the bird to talk, it doesn't. Every bird is an individual, and not every individual wants to communi-

Alex's Game

African greys are known to frequently possess and display a great love of tricks and games. The smarter the bird, the more potential it has to find ways to enjoy "tricking" humans. It would stand to reason, therefore, that Dr. Pepperberg's bird, Alex, probably knows a surprising number of tricks to play on humans. However, it hadn't occurred to me that a bird that lives in a university laboratory and that interacts daily with very intelligent, well-educated people would spend two days trying to trick me into breaking the rules.

As I awkwardly negotiated the disinfectant procedures, when visiting Alex, he could immediately recognize me as a newcomer, and "easy pickins" for mischief. Regarding me through first one oblong, slitty eye, then another, Alex bobbed his head and treated me to a loud, tonally correct wolf whistle. Both parts.

Then he stopped, looked again, and waited. I was just about to pucker up to respond with my own whistle when Dr. Pepperberg put her hand on my arm and shook her head "no."

Alex immediately repeated only the first half of the wolf whistle, regarding me with expectant mischief in his eyes. Again, Dr. Pepperberg shook her head "no."

You see, those who study Alex's language skills have decided not to engage in whistling with Alex in the laboratory because it might interfere with his desire to use human words which are more difficult to form. Newcomers are usually unaware of the rules, and Alex knows that they can sometimes be tricked into playing whistling games.

Again, and again during the few treasured hours I visited, Alex tried to "sucker" me into forbidden whistling interactions. It wasn't easy to ignore his charming, innovative, invitational whistles. It was extremely difficult to take Dr. Pepperberg's instruction, for Alex can be demanding in his quest for self-rewarding interactions. I guess he knows that all work and no play might make Alex a "dull boy." In fact, Dr. Pepperberg says that Alex is very dedicated in his quest for self-rewarding behaviors, spending many more hours playing than working.

cate with language. The only way to be absolutely guaranteed a talking grey parrot is to acquire a bird that is already talking. Sometimes this means looking for a young talking bird; sometimes it means acquiring a parrot that is mature. An exciting new home and an exciting new environment (even if they're simply a remodeling job) often bring new words and happy new behaviors into a mature bird's routines.

Chapter Five

What Does a Grey Parrot Really Need?

A safe cage in a secure location supports successful adjustment for these potentially sensitive birds. Physical components combined with social and behavioral elements can create an indoor habitat where a confident, well-socialized grey parrot thrives. The bird owner may need to encourage, perhaps even demonstrate, features of a new cage and other parts of the physical environment in order for the bird to reap the full benefits of well furnished surroundings.

Grey Haven

The best and the brightest parrot deserves the best equipment, and the cage is a very important part of that. Recent advances in cage design have brought us truly bird-proof latches and efficient mess catchers that contain both the mess *and* the bird. Today's premium cages are larger and stronger, often powder coated, occasionally stainless steel. Most are self-supporting units on wheels that can be easily

moved or cleaned. Most have three bowls (one each for water, dry, and moist foods), and many new cages now have a fourth bowl that is excellent for stowing foot toys.

The cage is the grey parrot's retreat. This is where the bird can relax and feel secure. No surprises occur here. There are toys to play with and food to eat. There are no demands made and no threats. The cage is a haven.

A well-adjusted grey is curious. Left outside the cage, the bird might decide to chew on an electrical cord, eat a poisonous plant, or take a dive into the toilet. A bird cannot be counted on to make wise decisions while traversing the human world. A cage provides physical as well as emotional security.

Baby's First Cage

A baby grey can easily have a bad reaction to the wrong first cage. The first cage should be small, safe, intimate. A very young grey in a too large cage might feel frightened or insecure. It might jump or fall off of the perch, scratch in the corner, or call in a high-pitched single tone. A newly weaned grey might refuse to eat independently and revert to handfeeding. It might even chew feathers—a true sign that something needs to change.

Cages with few horizontal bars are difficult for a young bird still struggling with coordination to climb. Young birds often seek security in small, closed places. A good-sized first cage for a baby grey parrot is probably about 20 × 20 × 28 inches (51 × 51 × 71 cm) with ¾-inch (19 mm) spaces between bars. A cage less than 18 inches (46 cm) deep might make a bird feel more exposed than protected because it cannot move back into the cage very far. To increase a shy bird's feeling of security, the top of the cage might be covered or partially covered with a gray towel extending down four or five inches (10 or 13 cm) on all sides. The bird can go up into the top for privacy in much the same way it might go up into a tree. Such a cage cover is best placed on the cage while the bird is not inside.

If you already own a large permanent cage for the new parrot, you might avoid the expense of a baby cage by raising the grate, making the part of the cage occupied by the bird smaller. Simply use self-locking cable ties (available in the electrical department of any hardware store) to secure the grate that came with the cage or a homemade grate or platform to higher horizontal bars.

Once the youngster begins developing confidence and independence, the grate can be lowered. If it's difficult or impossible to raise the grate, try lowering all perches within a foot or so of the grate, then gradually raise the perches as the bird's coordination and confidence increase.

A Permanent Palace

By the time a grey parrot is flying, it has usually developed the confidence necessary to be moved to a permanent cage. A cage used only for "roosting" or sleeping at night doesn't have to be large. However,

the place where the bird entertains itself during the day must accommodate wing-flapping space, swinging space, and lots of toys. A cage about two feet deep by three feet wide by four feet high (61 × 91 × 122 cm), which probably makes the top five feet (152 cm) from the floor, is ideal. This is enough space for a grey parrot, Red-tail or Timneh, to feel both uninhibited and secure.

Each bird's emotional needs are also a factor in determining proper cage size. Some grey parrots do not feel secure in a too large cage. A small percentage of greys seem almost claustrophobic in a too small cage. An appropriate cage for one grey parrot might stimulate unwanted behaviors in another.

The cage must be usable as well as the proper size. Cages with horizontal bars facilitate climbing and exercise. While grey parrots can certainly climb up and down vertical cage bars if they want to, they must have more motivation to do so. Without horizontal bars, they will climb up and down less often and rely on walking back and forth on perches for entertainment. At least two sides of the cage—on the sides or the front and back—should have all horizontal bars. A cage with too few horizontal bars can contribute to sedentary behavior and lack of curiosity. Avoid round or cylindrical cages—even squared cages with rounded corners—as shy grey parrots find safety in cage corners.

Fabulous Features

The cage door should be large enough that the bird can sit comfortably on a hand (if it chooses to do so) without having to duck while going through. Passing through openings of any kind can be problematic for many birds. Having a large enough cage door can help prevent some individuals from being reluctant to go into or out of the cage on the hand; step-up practice can add to the bird's comfort in performing this procedure.

When selecting the optimum cage, consider the following:

The ease with which the cage can be serviced

Composition/material/finish. The most popular cages these days are powder coated. They stand up to the beak of an African grey and are very easy to clean. The bars can also be brass or chrome plated or stainless steel. Never use hardware cloth, as it is coated with zinc (which is toxic), or wood (the bird will reduce it to a pile of toothpicks).

Structure or design. The cage should be structured so that no openings or spaces between bars are large enough for the bird to put its head through or small enough to catch a toe. Ornamental wires or bars should usually be avoided. Birds will get legs or feet caught in bars that form a V, such as where the bars come together in a domed-top cage. Round cages tend to promote fearfulness. A grey feels much more secure if the flat backside of the cage is against a wall. Many grey parrots demonstrate an obvious preference for corners.

Bars on a good-quality cage are too thick for the bird to bend. Joints will be smooth. There will be no sharp edges within the parrot's reach. The cage will not be easy to disassemble, or the bird will take it apart. The finish cannot be flaky. Remember that the bird might live in this cage for 40 years or more.

Perches. Perches that come in the cage may or may not be suitable for either a Red-tailed or Timneh grey parrot. Many larger cages come with hardwood perches that are size-appropriate for much larger birds such as cockatoos and macaws. These perches are often too large for a grey to grip; as you are probably well aware by now, the grey parrot loves to grip the perch and flap. Both hand-held and stationary perches should be provided in a variety of easily gripped sizes. For the bird to be able to grip the perch, opposing long toes must extend at least a little more than halfway around. Soft wood branches, such as those of any of the poplar family, are suitable perching surfaces as long as much of the bark is intact. Plum and citrus are also excellent perch material. Manzanita, dowel rods, "grooming" perches, and plastic or PVC perches and like materials are too hard and too smooth. A grey parrot's feet were designed to stand on branches with bark. The skin on the bottom of the feet needs the texture of the bark to stay in good condition. Poor perches will cause soft or worn spots to form

should easily accommodate this activity. If a cage-top perch is used, be sure that the highest point where the bird can sit comfortably is also easily gripped for strenuous flapping.

Trays and grates. The cage should also be easy to clean, with a removable tray and, preferably, a removable grate. Grey parrots like to play on the bottom of the cage and a grate will keep them from playing in their droppings and any old food that can be a disease risk. The bars of the grate should be as close together as the bars in the rest of the cage.

Dishes. If the cage you like comes with aluminum dishes, replace them. Stainless steel or ceramic bowls are easier to clean and last longer.

Introducing a Grey Parrot to a New Cage

A grey parrot might be excited about moving to new quarters. On the other hand, if a bird has been in only one cage, such as a baby cage, its entire life, or if it has been in the same cage for many years, it could have an adverse reaction to a new cage or to the way it is introduced into the cage. Avoid forcing the move on the bird and provide motivation for a change of heart. Place the new cage in the position of the beloved old cage with the old cage beside it. Put favorite toys and treats into the new cage. If the bird freely

on the bottoms of the feet. These spots can become sores and cause serious problems for the bird. Branches from trees are less expensive and healthier for the bird. Remember to cut several so that there are spares and to scrub them with soap, bleach, and water and leave them in the sun to dry.

Note: African greys love to spend time on top of their cages holding on and flapping like crazy. The cage top

enters the new cage and seeks toys and food there, food and water can be removed from the old cage during the day. By the third or fourth day, if the bird is eating in the new cage, the old cage can have all toys and perches removed and can be set on the floor so that the bird will more or less have to "choose" the new cage.

Location, Location, Location

The caged location should stimulate feelings of comfort, safety, and security. A grey parrot likes to be in an area where it can experience the most interaction with its human flock members and still feel safe. Many greys live in dining rooms and living rooms, but a cage that is exposed on all sides will not seem secure, so avoid placing the cage in the middle of the room or against a window.

An "ideal" location for most African greys would be as high as the bird's disposition allows, against a wall, and across the room from entrances and heavy traffic areas. A bird located beside a high-traffic doorway could experience fear reactions whenever anyone rushes unexpectedly through. Shelter may be important to a grey parrot's sense of safety, and greys just love peeking out from behind plants and toys; however, height is probably the most significant factor in stimulating feelings of safety. If a particular grey parrot tends to be shy or fearful, that tendency can sometimes be improved by changing height.

The Roost Cage

Many grey parrots and the people who live with them benefit from having a separate cage for the bird to sleep in—a roost cage. This cage need not be large or fancy, for it is merely a quiet place to sleep in a dark, quiet area away from the hustle and bustle of evening activities. Ten to twelve hours of sleep per night are recommended for a grey parrot. A roost cage can help fill this need for a quiet place to sleep. The baby cage that the bird came home in is probably perfect for this purpose. This familiar second cage is also good for vacations, trips to the veterinarian, and other longer outings.

Height and Attitude

Height manipulations can stimulate changes in a parrot's attitude. A grey parrot may be noticeably sensitive to height, which can stimulate feelings either of territorial aggression, in a bold bird, or insecurity, in a shy bird. Shy greys might find comfort in being housed low, while outgoing birds might not tolerate it. A territorial bird might defend a position of control whether it is a cage door, a food bowl, or someone's shoulder.

Although we can begin with an assumption that height may be causing territorial aggression, trial-and-error changes might demonstrate that the reverse is true. Aggression may be difficult to distinguish from fear because of the grey parrots' well-developed fight-or-flight response, especially the first part of the fight-or-flight response—fear biting. Either raising or lowering the height of a nipping bird might bring a feeling of safety and eliminate the need to nip. Additionally, a shy bird may experience enhanced confidence by merely raising the height of the cage or the perches customarily used.

If a bird is starting to nip, implement changes to prevent the reinforcement of biting into a pattern. Avoid situations where biting is likely to occur by using a perch to pick it up through the door of the cage, not allowing shoulder access, and removing or replacing food dishes only when the bird is away from the cage or playstand.

On the Shoulder

Anyone might be bitten trying to remove a grey parrot from the shoulder, but height is not the only factor here; some of it has to do with the inability to make eye contact when the bird is there. Any bird with a well-patterned step-up response will usually step up with eye contact. Without eye contact, the pattern is not repeated, and the bird may choose not to cooperate. Although it is probably less dangerous to humans to allow a grey parrot on the shoulder than other larger hookbills, we do not recommend it except in situations where a frightened bird may need the extra sense of security, perhaps in an unfamiliar place.

Additionally, allowing a grey parrot on the shoulder is potentially

A grey parrot on the shoulder can easily injure a person's face and destroy jewelry.

dangerous to the bird. The floor can be a long fall, and grey parrots occasionally incur split breast injuries in such falls. Fear of falling can also be harmful to the bird's personality.

Change and Control Issues

An African grey parrot can become excessively concerned with control of its cage territory. This tendency to avoid anything unfamiliar is probably slightly greater in Red-tailed greys than in Timnehs. A grey parrot's environment should be regularly, sensitively altered. This is an important part of early socialization. Lack of planned, appropriate changes can damage a grey parrot's personality. If a young grey is not socialized early to tolerate reasonable, interesting changes, ill effects on behavior may be evident by the time it is one year old. We can reduce aggression and enhance the bird's sense of safety during changes by conditioning the bird to tolerate having its cage and play areas moved at least a couple of times yearly. This could mean merely reversing the position of the cage and the play area. It could mean moving it to other locations in the home, or it might mean simply rearranging toys and perches in the cage. Grey parrots can be extremely intolerant of human intervention in the arrangement of cage accessories. These birds' toys or perches should be rearranged only when the bird is out

of sight of the cage. Occasional introduction—at least three times yearly—of new and differently configured branches will provide interesting new perspectives for a happy, confident, nonaggressive bird.

Any change of scenery can reduce boredom and promote curiosity. A grey parrot might benefit from being moved from one room to another. If a particular bird gets nervous in another room or is unaccustomed to experiencing new surroundings, make changes gradually. The person in whom the bird has the most confidence should be the one to show the new room to the parrot. If the bird becomes anxious or fearful, don't force it to stay in the new room. The bird will gradually allow longer visits to new places, unless it feels trapped. In that case a panic reaction can result, so it's best to try to read the bird's mood and retreat before it gets too upset. Sometimes allowing the bird to visit the new place while enclosed in the safety of a familiar, comfortable carrier helps the bird bypass the feelings of insecurity it might have outside the carrier.

Chances are, most parrots will not live out their lives in one household. Most people do not live in the same house for 50 or 60 years. If a parrot is allowed to develop a very narrow sense of secure places, it could be devastated when a move becomes necessary. A bird that is carefully introduced to unfamiliar places will become more open to going to other new places and will thrive when inevitable changes occur.

Chapter Six
Battling Boredom

The companion grey parrot's ancestors evolved a metabolism equipped to cope with a life of danger and independence. Almost all indoor environments are missing important elements such as provision for flying, foraging, and nest site preparation that the wild bird would access. These activities enable the bird to express energy that results naturally from its metabolism. Unused energy, as in a wing feather-trimmed companion bird sitting in a cage ("couch potato"), is frequently expressed as displaced, usually inappropriate behaviors. Unexpressed nervous energy can appear as fearfulness, screeching, or feather destructive behaviors.

In the wild, the bird would be physically and intellectually challenged by activities related to survival. No food and water bowls sit on the end of the branch, so the wild parrot spends most of its time foraging for food. In captivity, both food and water are only footsteps away. Effective strategies must be formed to help the bird use the energy that would be used during foraging in the wild.

Exercise

A captive bird can't possibly get as much exercise as it would get in the wild where it typically flies miles for a meal. Young greys are quick to start practicing and getting into shape for the flying they anticipate. They will stand on the door of the cage or perch where they can flap unfettered. They will, on their own, flap until they are out of breath. Many greys, shortly after fledging, will discontinue this type of exercise voluntarily and need to be encouraged to continue. Greys that haven't done it in years may have to be sensitively "reminded" of the benefits of activity.

Exercise helps relieve stress and boredom in birds just as it does in humans. It improves circulation and the flow of oxygen throughout the body. Much of a grey's self-confidence comes from knowing its wings will "work" and feeling the resistance of air against wing feathers.

Check the state of the wing feathers before expecting a companion grey to want to flap. Many birds that are actively growing in feathers are very protective of them and will refuse to risk breaking them by flapping. Some greys will even want to stay in their cages to make sure they won't have to flap. A grey with actively growing primary feathers should not be asked or required to flap against its will.

A young grey parrot may be encouraged to exercise by slowly rotating the hand it is perched on. The bird will flap to maintain balance. Some older greys will give up on flapping and simply hold on tighter to the hand. Moving your hand up and down can be a little stronger encouragement. For greys having a hard time getting an exercise program started, you can try holding the bird about two or three feet (61 to 91 cm) over a bed and sensitively causing the bird to fall from the hand or arm onto the soft mattress.

Once a parrot gets the idea, it will enjoy, perhaps even solicit, the exercise and look forward to doing it regularly. A healthy grey probably needs to flap until it is breathing hard at least once daily. If this activity seems to be causing extensive hard breathing or seems to be causing rather than relieving stress, it's time for a trip to the veterinarian.

Rainfall and Bathing

Wild greys spent thousands of years, hundreds of generations, evolving a metabolism enabling

them to function fully in the rain. That means that grey parrots can forage for food, nest, reproduce, feed, and raise young while they are wet. Rainfall is missing in the companion setting, and all the energy birds need to survive wet is unused.

Some of the lost opportunities to express energy and to burn calories and frustration can be replaced by treating the bird to frequent drenching showers. The energy expressed by bathing and recovering from being wet helps to prevent some of those temper tantrums that can occur so frequently in captivity.

Grey parrots are famously reluctant to enjoy showers, although this can be easily learned from baby Amazons. Companion grey parrots are more likely to enjoy bathing in a bowl; sometimes just a shallow bowl of water is enough. While this

Steps to Successful Showers

- Spray the bird while it is dipping its head into the water dish to bathe.
- Change the water temperature (warmer or cooler).
- Increase room temperature.
- Run the vacuum cleaner or other artificial waterfall sounds.
- Prime the bird for the shower by spraying a little, then coming back a minute later and spraying more.
- Alter the location where the shower is offered—on the cage, in the cage, in a playpen, etc.
- Change the time of day (earlier or later).
- Change the type of spray (smaller or larger drops) or appearance (color) of spray bottle.

is better than not bathing at all, it has some disadvantages:

1. The bird's back doesn't get wet, and those feathers can remain soiled.

2. Since the bird really doesn't get wet, it doesn't use the requisite amount of energy usually expended by a parrot that flies around in the rain, then later recovers from being wet.

3. The bird is likely to poop in the water, fouling both the water and the bird.

Showers can supplement and replace some of the bird's own bathing efforts. Sometimes, a quick shower just as fresh water is provided in the bowl will stimulate an immediate bath, and water can be replaced afterward.

Although companion grey parrots do sometimes enjoy sharing showers with their humans, regular showerheads are usually too harsh and forceful for most greys to enjoy. Some African greys also resist a spray-bottle shower; a particular bird may have to be conditioned to enjoy being sprayed. Hold the bottle, faucet-connected spraying device, or pump-up sprayer lower than the bird and spray a continuous mist over the bird's head so that the water falls down on the bird like rainfall. If the bird is reluctant to accept a shower, discontinuing eye contact when spraying may help. Sometimes demonstrating (modeling) enjoyment of the shower, possibly with another person or bird, can stimulate a grey parrot to accept the shower. If the bird is to be thoroughly wet, it's best to bathe in the morning so that there's ample time for the bird to dry naturally before nightfall.

Decisions, Decisions

A wild parrot is never bored. It must constantly search for food while existing in a state of danger. Many foraging activities involve decision-making processes: where to go, what part of the plant to eat, how to get back to the roost alive.

Trim long strands from well-used toys to avoid toe entanglement.

Parrots develop more stable personalities, more confident dispositions, from having access to appropriate choices—multiple environmental elements provided simultaneously. When many suitable toys and perches are available, no matter what is chosen, the bird tastes success: a happy, self-rewarding experience.

Toys and the Instinct to Destroy

Grey parrots are notorious for alleviating boredom with damaging activities. These cavity breeding birds need destructible accessories—branches, bark, wood, cork, paper, cardboard, cloth, leather, rope—the bird likes to destroy these items so they should be provided on a regular basis. A grey parrot without destructible accessories is like a dog without a bone. When those first new toys or perches are chewed up, mangled, or dismantled, frugal humans are tempted to replace them with indestructible ones. However, those items were destroyed because the bird's instincts *compelled* it to do so. Giving a grey parrot a toy that can't be chewed up, dismantled, or deconstructed is suppressing that retained instinctual wild behavior. Strong, sharp beaks exist for a reason, and if destructible elements are not provided, the bird

Grey parrots love leather knots!

ment of confidence and curiosity. Stress reduction and feelings of well-being combine to reinforce a continuation of these activities. This is common self-rewarding behavior. The more often the bird finds new things that can be used for self-reward, the more it will be compelled to find new things that can also be used in this way. It will begin investigating objects to determine which ones can be used as toys.

Humans are comfortable with the idea of giving toys to children and animals. Most recipients are happy to see toys and know immediately what to do with them; however, a grey parrot might suffer apathy in a cage filled with toys. You'd think a creature as smart as a parrot should be able to figure out how to play with a toy, but grey parrot intelligence depends upon its ability to learn new things and to apply already known concepts to new situations. For greys, curiosity and playfulness must be demonstrated by other birds, or by human caregivers.

Baby greys learn a great deal from their clutchmates. When two or three juvenile greys confront a foreign object, if the first bird encountering it expresses fear, the others will assume it is a scary thing and will copy the behavior. A grey that is raised with an Amazon—typically a more brazen, fearless bird—is usually less inclined to give in to its instinctual fight-or-flight response. A grey parrot raised with an Amazon will, more likely, learn to shred or attack an object in the manner

will find them. Harmful displacement behaviors will appear to accommodate that beak. The bird might simply begin destroying its own feathers. It might destroy its own personality or the trusting relationship between bird and humans.

What Is a Toy?

A toy is a tool for accessing self-rewarding behavior. It is designed to be enjoyable to use, even though it has no purpose other than the process of using it. The act of expressing pent-up natural behaviors on toys provides physical and emotional release promoting the develop-

demonstrated (modeled) by the Amazon. This applies to other activities as well.

At some point, the companion grey *must* learn to play with toys. Greys deprived of the luxury of learning from other parrots as they would in the wild must be taught by humans how to be birds.

Humans love to cuddle babies—any babies with skin, fur, or feathers. Like baby cockatoos that will lie in a person's lap soaking up constant affection, baby greys love to cuddle, snuggle, hug, and pet. While affection is important to a grey parrot, these types of displays do little to help the bird learn to function independently.

Showing Interest

There is no better way to get a grey interested in something than to let it see that someone else is so interested in it that it isn't shared. When introducing a toy to an African grey, pretend the bird isn't allowed to have it. Show it to the grey, but take it away before the bird has a chance to show that it's afraid of it. The "teacher" should be really excited about the toy. Show the toy to the bird briefly again, then give the toy to someone else who also shows excitement. Show it to the bird again. Give it to another bird, or to the dog, or to a child, while frequently showing it to the bird and taking it away again.

A grey parrot will start to lean toward the toy instead of away from it. At some point when the bird reaches out to tentatively touch it,

whisk the toy away again. When the grey becomes more insistent, and you think it will actually hold onto it, you can give the toy to the bird with much praise for agreeing to explore the new object. This keep-away game also works well with food.

To teach a grey to play with toys, humans must demonstrate whenever possible. Ripping paper, ringing bells, dragging pieces of rope around while the parrot is watching from a distance can stimulate the bird to copy these behaviors. For greys willing to still sit on a lap, placing toys in the lap, gently pawing at them and playing with them will help get the bird interested.

Encouraging Exploration

The handler might attach toys to a shirt where the bird will be likely to pick at them in the way it might pick at a button or jewelry. Spreading toys out on the floor and demonstrating playing can encourage exploration. An older grey might prefer to watch this display from a perch, while a younger one may insist on joining in. If the bird sees the human as a respected and important flock member, it will learn while watching.

Some greys grab and rip paper if it is perceived to be in the way. Once they discover that this is fun, they begin ripping more things. Placing paper pompoms in the cage next to a favorite perch or intrusively hanging down can stimulate the bird to experiment with these paper objects and, subsequently, toys in the same

Avoid toys with round "jingle" bells, which can entrap toes in the open slits.

locations. Watch carefully, especially with Timnehs, to ensure that the bird isn't actually eating the paper.

The following toys can be used to encourage playing:

- A piece of cheap box tape (the kind that isn't too sticky) wrapped around a chunk of cotton rope not more than 1.5 inches (3.8 cm) long, or around a strip of denim cut on the bias like shoestring tips.

- Wooden spoons.
- Pompoms made from newspaper or other plain, not shiny, paper.
- Cardboard tubes.
- Whole rolls of untreated, clean, unused bathroom tissue that has not been stored in the bathroom.
- Dull paper junk mail on a skewer made for birds or woven in the cage bars.

- Old jeans or cotton material cut into strips, on the bias so the strings aren't long, and tied to the cage bars or to other toys.
- Popsicle sticks.
- Paper cups or paper plates. Holes can be punched in them and straws woven through. Remember: Any rope or string given to the bird should be short enough to not accidentally wrap around the neck or feet.
- Plastic straws.
- Some plastic toys made for children; watch to ensure that the bird's toes and feet can't get caught in them.
- Avoid toothbrushes because the bristles of most, if not all, are anchored with tiny pieces of zinc, a metal toxic to birds.
- Favorite end tables, the arms of the chairs, and prized pieces of heirloom furniture (well, grey parrots *think* those make great toys!).

It's not unusual for humans to be proud of the fact that they don't have to worry about getting new toys all the time because their grey never chews things up. This should be considered a behavior problem to be addressed with corrective measures. While that particular bird may not have developed any problems the owner finds annoying, it cannot live for 50 years without entertaining itself in some way. If this is not done by chewing and playing with toys, it will probably be accomplished with screaming or feather mutilation.

Vocalization Games

A typical African grey enjoys artful vocal communication. Greys want to join in the conversations going on among other flock members. A companion grey picks up body language and the cadence of conversations and begins interjecting words and phrases such as *"Uh huh," "Okay," "That's right,"* in addition to well-timed chuckles.

Simply by talking to an African grey while performing daily rituals and labeling things that are part of the parrot's daily life, the bird will pick up language that will help it join in the flock's activities. The parrot benefits on many levels from this interaction. It learns to trust the owner who always lets it know what will happen next, it learns to ask for the things it needs and so gains self-confidence by being in control of certain aspects of life, and it is part of the flock because of being able to vocally join in.

Greys love to whistle. A human who lives with a grey can have great whistling contests with the bird. A grey parrot is capable of learning a whole song, but may prefer to do solos in the middle or join one song with another, or take pieces from many songs and piece them together. They are almost always grateful for input from their human companions. These jam sessions can go on and on, finally leaving humans doubled over in laughter.

Chapter Seven

Delivering a Proper Diet

iet is the first step in preventing and solving all health and behavior problems. Although African greys can be finicky, as a spoiled child might be, most are naturally *very* food-focused and will eat almost anything. Sometimes, picky eating becomes a game, a game of who trains whom. Many parrots remain on poor diets because some owners mistakenly believe that since there have been no health problems, the diet must be okay. Because of the grey parrot's ability to look good even when it doesn't feel good, that may or may not be true.

What and What Not to Feed

In general, both nutrition and eating habits—how to promote good habits and discourage bad ones—are equally important. Consider the following when planning a parrot's diet:

- A parrot's nutritional needs are not much different from those of a human.

- Vitamins obtained through food sources are more useful and less dangerous than chemically added vitamins.
- The best way to supply a variety of nutrients is to supply a variety of foods.
- A grey will not automatically eat nutritious food. Instead, when offered a large amount of food, it will select what it likes best.
- Some birds, when consistently offered a large amount of food, will eat for recreation and not develop more healthy ways of entertaining themselves.
- Parrots often resist change.
- Good habits are easiest to establish at an early age.
- Parrots will use the "flock" around them as a role model for what to eat.
- Excess fat, preservatives, and artificial ingredients are not good for birds.

Many of these points may seem familiar since most also apply to humans and other warm-blooded animals. Unfortunately, getting proper nutrition into a grey is not as simple as mixing the proper proportions of ingredients and putting them into a dish. You must also ensure that the nutrients are actually getting into the bird in the proper proportions.

Avian nutrition deserves volumes on its own. Consider investing in a book on this subject. As an overview, the following tips should be helpful in devising a suitable diet for your grey.

Vegetables: Vegetables are the best source of vitamins and minerals. They can be served fresh, thawed, raw, or lightly cooked. If one-third to one-half of a grey parrot's diet consists of carefully selected vegetables, many of the requirements for vitamins and minerals will be met. Some vegetables contain many more nutrients than others. Sweet potatoes, carrots, yellow squash, collard or dandelion greens, kale and broccoli (sources of calcium), chard, beets and beet tops, and peppers (green or hot) are especially good sources of vitamins A, K, and E. Other good vegetable choices include peas, green beans, leaf (rather than head) lettuce, lima beans, navy beans (also good for calcium), various types of sprouts, celery, zucchini, and cucumbers.

Please note that corn does *not* appear on this list. Corn is not a vegetable (it's a grain), nor is it a good source of vitamins or minerals, *and* it is high in calories. Any parrot can easily fill up on corn and avoid eating more nutritious selections.

Pellets: Another one-third to one-half of the diet can be comprised of high-quality pellets designed for companion parrots. Extensive

research has gone into developing diets that will deliver balanced nutrition in every bite. Since the birds cannot remove some of the nutrients from the chunks and eat others, the pellet can help fill in the nutritional gaps. Pellets also make it easier to maintain balanced nutrition of the bird's diet on those days when you are in a hurry and cannot prepare a normal meal. It is also nice to be able to let the pet-sitter feed pellets for a few days when you're on vacation, rather than trying to teach a novice how to chop the proper balance of vegetables.

While there are many brands of pellets on the market, they are not all equal. Some have artificial colors and flavors, which, in a few instances, appear to have contributed to feather plucking. Some provide nutrition only through chemical additives, which are not always easily utilized by the body. Some appear to contain proper amounts of protein, but the protein may not be digestible or may not contain the proper variety of amino acids. Some have more natural ingredients, then taint them with preservatives. Some just taste bad. You should probably be willing to taste your bird's food. If *you* wouldn't eat it, the bird probably won't eat it either.

Assessing the quality of the pellet is easiest by reading the label. Much of the nutrition should be derived through food sources, such as

grains, some seed, alfalfa, kelp. Organic food sources are preferable. Brands in which there are only two or three food sources and a long list of chemical additives should be avoided.

Supplementing

Although many pelleted diets claim to be the only food the bird needs, there are behavioral and nutritional advantages in supplementing with fresh natural foods as described here. The best way to get a variety of nutrients into a grey parrot is by offering a variety of foods in addition to pellets.

One effective way to convince a bird to eat a variety of foods is to incorporate them into the human diet and share with the bird. These food choices must be made carefully. Offer fruits such as papayas, mangos, cantaloupe, pomegranates, apples, and bananas. Almonds have calcium. Corn bread, pasta, spaghetti (with sauce), pizza, small amounts of Swiss cheese or yogurt, cooked potatoes or rice, well-cooked chicken on the bone, soup (not hot!), chili, stir-fry, cereal, as well as many other foods, make good selections, presuming they are low in salt and fat. A parrot usually wants to eat whatever it sees its owner eating. Many people eat a healthier diet because they own a parrot.

Amount

Sometimes a bird will gorge on such less than nutritious "extras" as pizza or corn. Use the bird's head as a judge of proportion. If the bird is

being offered a portion that is the size of its head, ask yourself if you would eat a human head-sized portion of that food—or half that. Table foods should probably comprise less than 20 percent of a bird's diet.

A cooked mixture of soaked then cooked dry beans and grains is an easy-to-use source of different proteins. A large batch can be prepared and divided into portion sizes for freezing. Adding chopped sweet potatoes and other vegetables to the mix increases vitamin content.

Healthy Habits

If it could, an African grey might spend its whole day sifting through its food dish and rechewing the veg-

etables it already ate. Most babies start out doing this. A weaning grey should have many food choices available most of the time, but once the bird is weaned and maintaining its weight with solid foods, it's time to work on healthy eating habits.

Eating Times

Parrots, presuming they are healthy, have two primary eating times and do not need food available at all times. Morning is the biggest mealtime of the day. This is often the best time to offer vegetables and soft foods such as cooked grains. Pellets and small amounts of table food can be offered in the evening. Grey parrots should not be fed so much at each meal that they cannot finish it.

Most foods that are good for people to eat are suitable for feeding to birds, but these may not be good nutritional choices. Many veterinarians now suggest pellet-only diets because so often the fruits, vegetables, and table food a bird owner feeds turn out to be the low-nutrition choices of apples, corn, and french fries.

- Avocados and chocolate are toxic and should not be fed.
- Caffeine, alcohol, and junk food (foods with high percentages of fat, sugar, or salt) must be avoided.
- Stale food, old seed, "honey sticks," moldy produce, and other foods that would be rejected by most humans are also unacceptable for birds.

Many parrot owners want to be kind to their bird by leaving food available for him at all times. They are worried that the bird might become hungry; however, being hungry is not really a bad thing. In the wild, hunger would motivate the bird to go find his next meal. Leaving food available at all times encourages bad habits such as picky eating and not playing with toys because he is playing with food instead and, if soft food is left in the cage, it may be spoiled when the bird goes to chew on it later. A grey that is fed smaller amounts will eat its favorites and throw the rest to the ground. Many birds finish their morning meal within a few hours. This doesn't mean that the dish must be refilled.

One way to provide food as well as mental stimulation during the day is to put chunks of raw vegetables in "foraging toys," that is, toys designed to make a bird work for the food.

Most birds would probably choose to eat again in midafternoon, maybe around 3:00 or 4:00 P.M. They can learn to wait a few hours later if necessary. If you will be coming home very late, a small amount of dry pellets, which won't spoil, can be left in the cage. This should be discontinued if the bird becomes reluctant to eat the variety of food offered.

Mealtime is a social time for greys as for many other types of parrots. The bird will expect to eat at the same time as you and will want to be able to see the rest of the "flock" eating. Often, a good way to get a grey to eat new foods is to eat them in front of it, or to feed the new food to another "flock member" who visibly enjoys it. Merely wanting to join in the "flock's" activity will often be enough to encourage the naturally inquisitive grey to try something new.

Dishes: Provide two sets of food and water dishes so that the bird can begin each day with clean bowls. Water dishes should also be washed whenever the water is dirty. (Some greys like to soak their food.) If a grey is really bad about soaking food or dumping water, supplement that bird's water supply with a drinking tube so that the bird will always have clean water.

Special Needs

Some greys may have low blood calcium, which can lead to seizures and other medical problems. For this reason, it's a good idea to feed calcium-rich foods such as kale, broccoli, Swiss chard, and almonds. Some people supplement calcium with cuttlebone or mineral block in the cage, but many birds chew these up without really swallowing any. Also, cuttlefish can accumulate heavy metal toxins if they come from polluted waters.

A grey's blood calcium level should be checked during its yearly health exams. An experienced avian veterinarian can help to determine what, if any, food supplements might be needed. Don't supplement either vitamins or minerals without a veterinarian's supervision.

Changing a Grey Parrot's Diet

A grey with unhealthy eating habits probably falls into one of these categories:

1. It recognizes only seed as food and will eat nothing else.

2. It has eaten the same few food items for most of its life and is unwilling to try anything new.

3. It has decided what foods it likes and will have temper tantrums or hunger strikes until the owner gives it the food it wants.

Birds in the first category cannot be "starved" into eating something they don't consider food any more than a human could be starved into eating marbles. The goal is to get the birds to realize that other things can be eaten. Sprouting their seed is often a good start. Cooking their seed into "omelets" of half egg and half minced vegetables, or into corn bread that has vegetables in it can encourage them to experiment. Gradually, the seed can be reduced and other ingredients increased in

toys can be helpful. Also, putting made-for-birds skewers with chunks of vegetables near the favorite perch gives the bird a good opportunity to try them. A nearly foolproof method involves replacing the bird's regular food with a new food item for one of their two daily meals every other day. Only one out of four meals is comprised of the new food item, so the bird will be in danger of not eating really well only at those meals and in no danger of starving.

Some birds have eaten properly in the past, but are manipulating their owners to give them their favorite food items. Usually, these birds have owners who just want their birds to be happy, so, to accomplish this, they give the bird too much food. Quite often, reducing portions will convince the bird to eat a balanced diet. This is sometimes more effective if the owner feeds the bird, then goes to work so that he or she need not endure the tantrum.

The bird's weight must be monitored daily when doing dietary changes. Work on a bird's diet only if it is healthy. It is very dangerous to assume that a bird will give in and eat if it is hungry. Extreme changes in the diet may take a year to effect.

size and quantity. Cooked sweet potatoes or squash or vegetable baby food can be mixed with the seed. Again, other ingredients can be added gradually.

Once the bird is experimenting with new food, or if it is in the second category, the owner can encourage better eating habits by eating in front of the bird and sharing. The game for introducing new

Chapter Eight
Grooming Greys

A parrot relies on nails, beak, and/or wing feathers in everything. The bird needs to know that these body parts are going to perform adequately or its ability to function as a bird is compromised, possibly leading to serious behavior problems. Grooming the nails, beak, and wings is necessary at times, but this must be done sensitively. The bird needs to be handled gently during the process and the grooming itself must still allow the bird to function in its environment.

Whether it's a result of grooming or the process of grooming, inappropriate trimming of wings, nails, or beak can damage a grey, especially a baby, physically, emotionally, and behaviorally. Either wings or nails that are too short can cause the bird to fall and crash, which can lead to feather disorders, including damaged wing feather follicles and, in extreme cases, skin broken open over the breastbone.

The following techniques are intended to be minimally invasive, both in the process of grooming and in the effect of grooming, on the bird's future confidence and on its ability to comfortably regrow feathers. Even low-stress grooming can

be scary for the bird the first time, however, and conditioning to tolerate grooming is an important part of being a responsible parrot owner.

To Trim or Not to Trim?

Whether or not to trim wing feathers is a decision that must be made on an individual basis. In some households, allowing the bird to fly is a possibility, and in other homes it is not. There are risks and benefits to both lifestyles that each owner must carefully weigh before making a choice. In some places it is illegal to trim a bird's wing feathers. In these places the home must be set up to minimize dangers to the flighted bird.

Both flighted parrots and those with trimmed wing feathers have advantages and serious disadvantages. These must be carefully weighed before making a decision as to which lifestyle suits both the parrot and his owner.

Many people trim wing feathers so that the bird will not fly away. However, many birds with trimmed feathers still manage to fly away or

birds may express energy in ways that the owner finds problematic, such as screaming or biting.

Since a trimmed parrot can never fly away, it is more inclined to feel "trapped," possibly accounting for phobias and feather destructive behaviors that occur more commonly in trimmed birds.

Unflighted birds get much less exercise than flighted ones and this *cannot* be compensated for by allowing the bird to walk around. Flying stimulates the metabolic, circulatory, and respiratory systems. The owner of a trimmed bird must spend time encouraging the bird to flap its wings daily to aid circulation and express energy.

Flying is a bird's main mode of getting around. Removing this can seriously compromise a bird's self-confidence. Removing this before it has learned to use its wings may result in the bird being crippled in this regard. A bird that passes the age where it would normally learn to fly and to properly use its wings may never be able to learn this later.

A parrot that flies regularly is a healthier bird. Anyone who watches a bird play in the air would argue that it is also "happier." Many behavior problems, including feather destructive behaviors, are regularly resolved by allowing the bird to experience flying.

A flying bird must be watched carefully while out of the cage. Some simple training is required to let the bird know where it may perch and where it may not perch. The owner

into something if they are scared enough or if a strong enough wind comes up. A trim that is so short that the bird cannot possibly fly leaves it in danger of injury if it falls during normal activity. No bird should ever be denied the ability to glide safely down.

The owners of trimmed birds may develop a false sense of security, thinking that the bird will stay on the play area while they leave the room to do something in another part of the house. Even trimmed birds can wander and get into trouble. Trimmed

must commit to making sure that doors are shut, and that the bird is either familiar with all of the windows and mirrors or that they are covered so that it will not crash into them. While the bird is learning to fly, it will have a lot of crash landings and all breakables should be removed from the area. Flying outdoors or in unfamiliar indoor locations is risky and should be undertaken only with a bird that is exceptionally dependable about flying exactly where it is prompted to fly.

Dangerous Situations

These can occur in the lives of both flighted or non-flighted birds. A grey parrot experiencing either lifestyle can die as a result. Deciding whether to trim or not to trim must be made by the bird owner based on circumstances and abilities. Either way, there will be inevitable "finger pointing" and "that wouldn't have happened if..." from proponents of the other side, if unwanted consequences occur.

Low-stress Grooming

It is possible to condition a bird to wing trimming without needing a towel. This is an ideal situation and is not nearly as difficult as it may sound. The key is to not expect too much and to provide praise at each step. The first step would be holding the scissors where the bird can see them. Touching scissors to feather may not happen for 10 or 20 steps.

Scissors should be sharp so that they leave as smooth an edge as possible on the trimmed feathers, to avoid potential feather chewing intended to "fix" jagged feather edges. Depending upon the bird's age and flight ability, trim only four to seven of the outer primary flight feathers. It's usually best to trim four feathers in younger birds and up to seven feathers in hearty older birds. Gauge cuts based on how much of the feather extends out of the shorter covering feathers or coverts. For baby greys, trim away about one-third of the part of the first four flight feathers extending beyond the coverts. Older birds and better flyers may require trimming up to two-thirds of the visible part of the first seven primary feathers extending past the coverts when the wing is viewed from above or behind.

The Least Invasive Trim

The bird's safety is the primary goal of wing feather trimming; the bird's comfort is the secondary goal. That's why we no longer use trims developed for the poultry industry, such as uneven trimming—cutting all primaries on one wing close or under the coverts and leaving the other wing full—for companion birds. This leaves the bird uncomfortably unbalanced and makes the simple activity of holding onto the top of the cage and flapping difficult and uncomfortable. Young birds, especially, that are trimmed this way may tend to fall in an uncontrolled

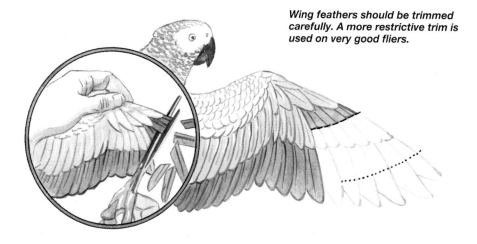

Wing feathers should be trimmed carefully. A more restrictive trim is used on very good fliers.

manner more than symmetrically trimmed birds. Older birds that have been trimmed this way for a long time tend to be inactive, a condition that can contribute to many other physical and behavioral problems.

Secondary feathers should be left intact to retain wind resistance so that the bird is able to land, dive, or fall safely. This is an indoor trim for maximum comfort for indoor birds. Birds trimmed as suggested here should be unable to lift off indoors, but not outdoors. No wing trim should be trusted outdoors where a strong gust of wind can blow even a severely trimmed bird away. Many birds can fly with the first two or three primaries left intact. If the idea is to keep the bird from flying, then these feathers should be trimmed.

Low-stress grooming also includes protecting the bird's ability to easily regrow feathers. While some birds seem to tolerate and recover from short trims, other birds have disastrous results. Wing feathers that are trimmed up to or under the coverts are especially vulnerable to being knocked out as they molt and regrow one at a time. Each individual blood feather has no protection as it grows past the coverts and can be bent or broken by the simple act of flapping.

Birds with feathers trimmed under the coverts or clipped at the base may experience regrowth problems. Without the protection and support of (at least partial) feathers on each side, each primary blood feather can be repeatedly broken or knocked out when it grows past the coverts. When these birds flap, the end of the wing will hit the perch or side of the cage instead of the feathers, since the feathers are completely missing. The wing can be bruised and even bloody.

Note: Feather cysts are usually the result of trauma where the

*Mature primary feathers protect
new feathers as they grow in.*

feather grows curled inside the follicle. This can be painful for the bird and can also progress to an inability to regrow these feathers. This condition can produce a sedentary bird that prefers not to use wings, a bird that chews feathers, or a bird with a phobic or aggressive personality. Inappropriate cage or perches, and overgroomed nails, can also contribute to this painful condition.

Some groomers claim that they "round" the cut end of feathers cut beneath the coverts with special scissors so that this will not happen. However, the large shaft of a grey parrot's primary flight feathers is hollow near the body (under the coverts), like a straw. It is not possible to "round" the end of a cut straw. Many people who thought their bird stopped chewing on feathers when cut in this manner later learn that the bird still chews feathers; they just couldn't see it because damage is hidden by the coverts.

Toweling

While most companion grey parrots will tolerate having the wing feathers groomed without toweling, it may become necessary to wrap the bird in a towel for medical examination or for grooming toenails or beak. If a companion bird has been well conditioned to playing "peek-a-

boo" in the towel, then necessary toweling is tremendously easy.

1. If you have been practicing with your bird, begin as you would for the towel game. Otherwise, place the bird on a waist-high perch and approach from below rather than from above as an avian predator would. Approach the bird slowly with the towel. If it looks as though the bird might jump off the perch, then back away a bit. Aim for picking up the foot. Before advancing, make sure the bird is reasonably comfortable. Give the bird

*Unprotected blood feathers can break
as they grow in.*

2. Once the bird is settled, hold it around the neck with one hand, carefully joining the thumb and opposing finger (outside the towel) just under the lower beak. Even if there is a little space in the circle formed by the fingers, if the fingertips meet directly beneath the beak and behind the jawbone, the bird is restrained, and cannot move.

3. Hold the bird's feet with the other hand, being careful not to restrict the in-and-out movement of the breast (a bird has no diaphragm and cannot breathe if the chest cannot expand).

4. Once the bird is safely restrained in the towel, a second person can examine the bird, groom wing feathers, toenails, or beak, or perform any other necessary procedure.

Grooming Toenails

Although it's extremely important to allow baby greys to have sharp toenails so that they won't fall often and develop related physical and behavioral problems, some grey parrots require frequent toenail grooming. An adult grey parrot's toenails should be kept so that the ball under the end of the toe is not displaced off a flat surface by the tip of the nail.

Some birds may be socialized to allow a favorite person to file the tips off the toenails with an emery board, but many birds will have to be toweled to have toenails groomed, even by a professional groomer or avian veterinarian.

something to do, such as "bite the towel." Once you have the bird's foot, use the same slow and careful technique to wrap it inside the towel. Continually give the bird the opportunity to calm down. Dimming the lights may help, although some birds are more comfortable if they can see what is going on.

Most professionals probably prefer a Dremmel tool for grinding African grey toenails. The heat produced by the spinning of the grinding stone can cauterize the blood supply in the toenail as the nail is being groomed, thereby minimizing the risk of bleeding. Occasionally, however, there is a little blood, and care must be taken to ensure that the bleeding is stopped. Use cornstarch or coagulating powder rather than a styptic powder because it is less painful.

Grooming the Beak

Grooming the beak is probably the most stressful part of grooming any parrot and is not necessary in normal circumstances. Occasionally, grey parrots suffer growth deformities of the beak. This may involve a maxilla (upper beak) growing to one side and a mandible (lower beak) growing to the other, rather than maxilla and mandible being centered over each other. This condition requires beak reshaping, which must be done gradually and by a professional. Never allow anyone except an experienced professional groomer or veterinarian that the bird tolerates well to use a Dremmel on a grey parrot's beak.

Stress-related Seizures

Fear and stress can cause seizures in parrots. Seizures during grooming

A toenail that lifts the end of the toe off of a flat surface should be trimmed.

are, apparently, increasingly common. They occur more often in birds requiring beak grooming. Jardine's parrots are particularly prone to getting heavily overgrown beaks, and seizures may be more common in them for this reason.

What does a seizure look like? It may be difficult for the bird owner to know if their bird is having a seizure while it is being groomed; some people can't discern a seizure even when it is pointed out in process. The head jerks at rhythmic intervals. The eyes stare blankly. Usually the bird is wrapped in a towel when this happens; if it weren't, it would be unable to stand. Or if it does stand, it cannot perch and must use the tail to balance. The most dangerous aspect of a seizure is that it can cause the bird to regurgitate and it may not be able to get the vomit out of its throat in order to breathe, possibly leading to death.

What causes seizures? One of the biggest stresses for a bird (or anyone, for that matter) is to feel trapped and to have no control over what happens. Chasing, "pouncing," or throwing a towel over the bird or otherwise taking it by surprise are usually the first steps that lead to seizures. Trying to get the grooming over quickly without regard to the bird's stress level is another. It seems intuitive that if grooming is causing stress, then it would be better to do it quickly, and then the bird spends less time being stressed. Actually, just the opposite occurs. Soon the bird will start having seizures before you can even get it into the towel.

How do I prevent seizures from ever starting? The most significant thing the owner can do is to make the process of wrapping the bird in a towel easier. The owner can hold the bird close to the chest with one hand over the back so that the handler can come in behind with a towel and the bird can be calmly transferred. Spend some time getting the bird used to being in a towel or having hands around it. Don't force these interactions, but praise the bird effusively for each little step it allows.

Choose a groomer who pays attention to how the bird is doing and who will recognize and stop when the bird is stressed. If the bird gets tense, stop whatever part of the grooming you are at and let the bird calm down before moving forward. If the bird's beak needs to be shaped and it is scared of the sound of the grinder, take a minute to let it know it's okay. It may take only a few times of turning the grinder on and off and praising the bird in *between* to teach it that the grinder noise is not so bad after all. The same goes with touching the grinder to the beak or any other part of the process. Make sure to give plenty of praise rewards and, if the bird responds well, scratches on the head during the process.

Don't put off the grooming. The more work to be done, particularly on the beak, the harder it is on the bird. It's much easier to quickly maintain beak growth than to try and carve something that looks like a beak out of a long mass of overgrowth.

Provide the bird with tree branch perches that have bark on them and plenty of wood to chew. Fruit tree branches are excellent for helping to keep beak growth in check. Wood that is very hard and smooth will not help much.

What if my bird has already started having seizures during grooming? Be sure the groomer goes slowly and stays within the bird's tolerances. Be prepared to stop when the bird has had enough, even if the job is not finished.

Every time the bird shows it is tense, stop immediately and give it a chance to relax and calm down. Praise and comfort the bird with familiar noises. Condition the bird to respond to distraction cues, such as *"You're a pretty bird"* before grooming and use the cues during grooming.

Chapter Nine

Process of Elimination and Other Common Questions

African greys are surely the most fastidious of parrots. It's not unusual for a companion African grey parrot to refuse to defecate while inside its roost cage. A grey parrot might choose to eliminate in only one or two areas of the regular daytime cage, or it might not eliminate in any chosen territory at all. This behavior, like several others we've discussed here, is probably a result of the numerous predators that wild grey parrots must so carefully avoid.

It can be quite a shock when a new parrot owner suddenly notices that the bird has some sort of "protocol" for eliminating. That protocol will vary from bird to bird, but usually remains consistent in a particular grey parrot as long as that bird has no reason to change. Parrot behavioral consultants come across questions about the greys' elimination habits with great regularity. Following is a sample of these questions.

A grey parrot can be trained to poop when held over a particular surface, such as newspaper.

Why won't my grey parrot eliminate in the cage where it sleeps?

The cautious grey parrot is probably too smart to eliminate where it sleeps in the wild so that predators are not attracted to the roosting areas.

Will it hurt my grey parrot if I sleep too long?

If the bird is not free-fed, it will not be taking in food during the hours of human sleep. If the bird is given the same amount of food every evening, then about the same amount of waste will accumulate. Holding it a little longer shouldn't be a problem for a sleeping bird. If the bird develops a sense of safety, and humans sleep for very long periods, the bird will discontinue the fastidious behavior.

Why won't my grey parrot eliminate anyplace in the cage except where it naps?

A particular grey parrot probably naps during the day in a site close to where it forages. This may be perceived to be far enough from the roost to seem safe; it has been observed that grey parrots might fly 20 or more miles (30-plus km) daily to find food. In captivity, nap sites are probably less numerous and so it will be easily observable where the bird has chosen to eliminate.

What can I do to change this behavior?

There is usually no reason to change this behavior, except by exploiting it for potty-training the bird. If the bird is extremely fastidious and must remain caged for very long periods, it might benefit from the introduction of a roost cage inside a much larger daytime cage. Use different substrate in each cage so that the bird can easily determine a difference in the territory.

Can I potty-train my bird?

It's tremendously easy to reinforce natural, self-rewarding behavior, and eliminating is both natural and self-rewarding. It's probably quite a bit easier to potty-train a grey parrot than a puppy. However, the added responsibility of pooping appropriately to please the teacher (you) can stress the bird and adds the potential for harming the bird's personality.

Why add stress to an already complicated situation. The parrot's waste is water-soluble and not usually smelly. If you do decide to potty-train a companion grey, you can easily take advantage of the bird's natural instincts to eliminate in particular areas in accordance with your bird's preferences.

Watch to see where and when your bird usually poops, reward that behavior, and see what happens. It's common for a particular grey parrot to prefer a particular substratum, and Dr. Susan Clubb reports that newspaper with print is the best material to use to line the bottom of bird cages. The ink in the newspaper retards the growth of bacteria, fungus, and molds more than any other material tested. Newspaper is an ideal visual stimulus for teaching a grey parrot where to eliminate. If acceptable areas for eliminating are lined with newspaper, and if the bird is reinforced to eliminate when you hold it over newspaper, then the bird is well on its way to being "potty-trained."

When handling or playing with the bird in a place you do not wish soiled with droppings, watch for tail movements that might indicate that the bird wants to eliminate, or keep an eye on the clock and put the bird down for a few minutes every 20 or 30 minutes. A well-socialized bird might eliminate immediately when put down and immediately want to be picked up again. If this doesn't happen, stop eye contact and look for signs that the bird's interest has shifted from you and what you're doing to something else; maybe watch the bird wag its tail or preen for a few seconds, or bop on a bell, or take a drink. Be sure there's been a break in the intellectual and emotional connection with the bird. Wait a few minutes, then pick the bird up and solicit interaction, hold it over newspaper, and the bird will eliminate before becoming emotionally "connected" again.

If this doesn't occur, try waiting a few minutes longer before putting the bird down, leaving the bird down a few minutes longer, giving a small food treat before picking the bird up, or encouraging a little wing flapping just as you pick the bird up. Any one of these activities could stimulate a grey parrot to eliminate. Reinforce the bird with verbal praise when it does.

Within a very short time, possibly a few days or a week, the grey parrot of any age usually gets a strong notion of where it should and should not eliminate. Only the neighborhood dry cleaners and carpet cleaners will be disappointed.

Chapter Ten

The Doctor and the Grey Parrot

Whether it's an accident or illness, an emergency is the worst possible time to be looking for a good avian veterinarian. Taking the new bird for an immediate examination is an opportunity to see the doctor's practices, techniques, and rapport with the bird and with you. If it's your first time visiting an avian veterinarian, you'll find out about medical, grooming, and boarding services available for your new grey companion, and you'll find connections to numerous resources such as the local aviculture club, bird behavior consultants, magazines, and pet sitters, and a whole new "bird world" will be revealed.

Your bird might not *have to* see a doctor again for decades, or you might need one next week. Greys that are well cared for rarely become sick. Proper diet, clean, uncrowded conditions, exercise, fresh air, and a low-stress life allow the bird to maintain a healthy immune system and will help it to resist infections caused by common bacteria and viruses. Crowded birds with poor diets living in stressful conditions may have chronic disease problems, and very young and very old parrots are more susceptible to disease. Unweaned birds and newly weaned birds have less resistance to disease than mature birds with fully developed immune systems.

Choosing an Avian Veterinarian

Avian veterinary science is a rapidly expanding field. Avian veterinarians must frequently pursue continuing education in this field in order to practice it competently. Look for a board-certified avian veterinarian; there are more every year. Otherwise, look for a member of the Association of Avian Veterinarians. In most urban areas, an avian veterinarian will have a clientele that is more than 50 percent birds and/or exotics. Also ask if the veterinarian has taken a test showing proficiency in this area. Ask for references and check them.

The Well-bird Checkup

An initial examination allows the new parrot owner to be more confident of the bird's good health. Even if the bird comes from a reputable source, there are illnesses such as Psittacine Beak or Feather Disease that cannot be detected without diagnostic tests.

This is an excellent time for the veterinarian to become familiar with the individual bird. Although there are published standards defining normal for different kinds of birds, variations exist between individuals. The veterinarian will obtain valuable information about what is normal for a particular bird by seeing that bird when it is healthy.

An avian veterinarian might recommend annual or semiannual examinations for a particular bird. Regular examinations can help to identify health problems in early stages. This is particularly useful if you have only a few birds and might not otherwise be in regular contact with a veterinarian. The veterinarian remains familiar with the bird and potential issues can be identified through changes that occur too slowly for most people to notice.

Vaccinations

As avian medicine expands and progresses, new developments in prevention such as vaccines are beginning to become available.

There are several vaccines on the market, but some may be too new or risky for veterinarians to recommend. Others have proven safe and effective. Veterinarians may suggest vaccinations on an individual case basis; however, there are no standard immunizations suggested for African grey parrots.

Injuries

A minor injury such as a nicked toe or wing tip can be treated at home. Applying a weak solution of Betadine will keep the area from becoming infected. If there is much bleeding or if the injury involved another pet, a trip to the veterinarian is needed. Sterile gauze and slight pressure can be applied to a bleeding wound. Scratches from other animals usually require antibiotics.

If you suspect a broken bone or concussion, keep the bird as still as possible (it will go immediately to sleep in a dark box) and take it to an emergency facility. Do not try to stabilize the injured part, as this can make the injury worse.

Signs of Illness

African grey parrots' instinct to live in flocks dictates that they can look good no matter how bad they feel. This means that an African grey parrot can look perfectly healthy while harboring an illness that will not be revealed until later. Stress related to going to a new home can bring out symptoms of disease that had previously remained hidden. A bird owner has the responsibility to ensure that this new friend is healthy and robust. Anyone who purchases a parrot should insist on a health guarantee that allows enough time to visit an avian veterinarian and to obtain test results, usually from one to two weeks.

A wise parrot keeper monitors behavior, droppings, and weight to help determine a parrot's health. Changes in these three areas can indicate possible illness.

Behavior

Grey parrots have a relatively consistent general activity level. The bird will have napping, playing, and vocalizing times, as well as times when it is more affectionate. Noticeable variations in these patterns, particularly if the bird is more quiet and less active than usual, can indicate possible health issues. Some birds may seem more agitated or jumpy; some may be more affectionate when they don't feel well.

The best time to assess the bird's activity level is when no one is directly interacting or paying direct attention to the bird. In nature, predators watch sick or injured animals because they are easier to catch. If a bird were to act sick because of minor illnesses, it would not live to reproduce because preda-

What to Do Until You Get to the Veterinarian

1. A sick or injured bird should be kept warm and still so that the parrot can use its energy to fight the illness or heal its injury. A bird's body temperature is higher than ours, often around 105°F (40.6°C). Much of a bird's energy goes to maintaining this temperature. A covered cage with a heating pad under it or on the side is an excellent idea.

2. Save the newspapers from the bottom of the cage so that the veterinarian can assess the droppings.

3. Transport the bird in a carrier or a box with ventilation. If the bird is panting, the temperature in the carrier is too high.

tors would attack. Also, the other birds in the flock might drive an obviously sick bird away to prevent disease transmission to the rest of the flock. For these reasons, even a bird that doesn't feel well is likely to act normal when interacting with its human. In many instances, *only you* will be aware that something doesn't seem "quite right" about the bird.

Droppings

There are three parts to parrot droppings.

1. Normal feces (the "green" part) will appear homogenous, well digested, and wormlike. Feces should usually have a firm consistency and should contain no distinguishable pieces of food. Color may change with the food consumed. Fresh fruits and vegetables can make droppings loose and sloppy; this should not be mistaken for diarrhea. When a bird has pellets as the base of its diet, stools should return to normal consistency after a pelleted meal.

2. The white part of the droppings carries the nitrogenous wastes and is called the urates. The urates of a healthy bird will be separate from the other two parts and will be opaque white. Occasionally, the whites will be temporarily stained from something the bird ate. Lime green or mustard yellow could indicate liver problems. Kidney problems can keep the bird from properly forming urates so that the liquid part of the dropping is cloudy white. Any observable change in urates or feces lasting more than a

day or two is good reason to consult a veterinarian.

3. The third part of the stool is liquid urine. It is usually clear and colorless, although it can pick up some color along with the feces. The amount of urine varies with the amount of water contained in the food or the amount of water the bird has consumed. Stress can cause the bird to have droppings that consist only of clear fluid; this should

A swing that attaches at only one point is more enticing to a grey parrot, because it swings in many directions, not simply back and forth.

not be confused with diarrhea. Sometimes there will be more water in stools in summer because birds drink more water when the weather is hot. A change in the amount of liquid in the stool is probably no cause for concern unless it is extreme and ongoing.

Diarrhea in a parrot shows up as undigested food in the feces, droppings that do not have three distinct parts, and weight loss in the bird. Whenever you believe an African grey has diarrhea, you should take the bird to the veterinarian as soon as possible. True diarrhea generally requires medical attention if the bird is to survive.

Weight

Unless an African grey parrot is on a diet, any noticeable weight loss is cause for immediate veterinary attention. Determining whether or not a bird has lost weight cannot be done by looking at the bird or by holding it on your hand. The best way to determine weight loss is to weigh the bird in the morning before it eats. Otherwise, examine the bird's keel bone frequently. The keel is a flat bone that is attached perpendicular to the sternum, below the bird's crop. The bird's flight muscles are attached to this protruding bone. Flight muscles are the largest muscles in the bird's body; they accurately reflect the loss of muscle tissue that occurs when a bird loses weight.

Feeling the keel bone on a regular basis allows you to become familiar with the parrot's normal shape and physical condition. If the keel bone becomes more prominent, contact the veterinarian. If the keel bone gets harder to find due to surrounding flesh, the bird should probably (under veterinary approval) be fed less. If you are actually weighing the bird, look for a decrease of 10 percent or more. Birds do not go on diet and exercise programs of their own accord. Weight loss in a pet bird is a serious matter that requires an avian veterinarian's care and cannot be remedied by feeding the bird more.

If you suspect something out of the ordinary in your bird's physical condition, don't wait more than a day or two. If the bird doesn't improve, especially if it is getting noticeably worse, you should stop waiting and take the bird to the veterinarian. You know the bird better than anyone else. An experienced bird veterinarian will not always expect a bird owner to be able to describe specific symptoms and will trust your judgment, whether or not you can identify specific complaints. While a list of symptoms is extremely helpful in diagnosing a problem, it is not always possible to come up with one. It is safer to have the bird checked than to wait until it is too late.

It never hurts to call the veterinarian if you have a question concern-

Predictable Symptoms

1. Sneezing can indicate a sinus infection; the bird could be copying a human sneeze, or it could just be a reaction to dry air.

2. Regurgitating could be a crop infection or a sign of true love.

3. Feather plucking or chewing could have its basis in a medical problem or in behavior.

4. Coughing usually occurs shortly after someone in the house has had a cold. African grey parrots do not cough. They do, however, do an excellent imitation of a human coughing.

ing the parrot's health. It can be fatal to wait to see if the health problem will go away or if it will worsen.

Holistic Medicine

Traditional Western avian medicine sometimes falls short when it comes to subtle and difficult-to-diagnose health conditions in parrots. Many reliable aviculturists report that their birds have had their lives saved by acupuncture, homeopathy, or Chinese herbs.

Holistic medicine is targeted more to prevention than treatment. A strong body does not get sick. Companion parrots on a holistic regimen involving diet and low stress appear healthier and "happier." Additionally, if there is a disease present, holistic treatment is usually less invasive

Be sure to take the bird in a carrier to prevent unwanted incidents with other pets in the waiting area.

other way around. Many parrots may be more disease-resistant than their human companions. If a bird gets a cold at the same time as a human, it may be a coincidence due to environmental factors.

In general, different types of bacteria are infectious to birds than to humans. Both humans and birds can be affected by salmonella or *E. coli*, and both humans and birds can get ornithosis. Ornithosis, which was previously called psittacosis or parrot fever is caused by a bacterium called *Chlamydia psittaci*, and can be transmitted between humans and birds. Transmission to humans is extremely rare and usually is considered to be an occupational disease of those working around birds. However, persons with pneumonialike symptoms should tell their doctor that they own a parrot in order to assist in diagnosing this easily curable disease.

People who develop a sensitivity to dust, including dust associated with African grey parrots, can develop *hypersensitivity pneumonitis*. According to the American Lung Association this is an inflammation of the alveoli in the lungs. Prolonged exposure to an offending substance can cause scar tissue to develop in the lungs.

and, therefore, both less dangerous and less stressful to the bird. In places where it is available, holistic avian medicine is a viable alternative that can be seen to save lives.

Can Diseases Transmit Between Humans and Parrots?

Most illnesses cannot be transmitted from birds to humans or the

Chapter Eleven
Behavioral Issues

Greys—and many other parrots—share an incredible ability to allow humans to take on the roles of mates and flock members. Excepting imprinted animals, this is a fairly unique ability. The most effective way to help a grey adjust successfully to the human circle of life is to provide guidance, nurturing, and an appropriate environment. Unfortunately, misunderstandings and many other issues can manifest when humans and birds try to live together. Since we are the more adaptable of the two, it is up to us to design a suitable environment and interactions that are as understandable to the bird as possible.

Unfulfilled Needs

Grey parrots have evolved or developed the instinct to forage, nest, fight or flee, and develop flock and mate relationships. These innate, characteristic activities are influenced by seasonal and breeding cycles. A companion grey experiences the same drives, desires, and hormones as a wild parrot, and not being able to participate in these experiences can be stressful to the bird.

Filling those needs in captivity is virtually impossible, so acceptable (to the bird) replacements must be found. Simply coping with confinement to a house or cage, having to learn to self-reward—something wild parrots develop naturally—understimulation, overstimulation, and having to learn how to be a parrot from a totally different species are all challenging. These grey companions are first and foremost simply birds. It's a wonder they can cope at all.

That's why they call them "parrots."

The Way of the Parrot

The strongest and smartest greys get the best food, the best nest sites, and the mate of choice. These individuals are held in high regard by other flock members that watch and copy their behavior. A successful relationship between human and companion grey parrots casts the human as a role model, with the inherent responsibility of setting a good example for other members of the flock.

Humans gain status in a parrot's eyes when they take time to model, guide, and reinforce appropriate behavior. If a particular human doesn't spend at least a little time teaching the bird appropriate behavior, then the bird might not see that human as a valued flock member, and might try to drive that person away. This is an instinctual response. It's not unusual for a grey parrot to abuse anyone who appears to have lower status in flock "society." A grey parrot might instinctually mistreat shorter people—including children.

Cues, Rewards, and Reinforcement

Verbal (or vocal) cues in conjunction with body language are the easiest ways to reward a parrot. Greys can easily be conditioned to respond in predictable ways when certain words are used repeatedly in similar situations. Body language and tone of voice are frequently as important as using the words in context.

Yes, the phrase "*Good bird*" is a useful cue, but it must be spoken with as much meaning in the context of the interaction as possible. This is similar to a person watching "Star Trek" and listening to Klingons. We can pick up that a certain series of sounds signifies the end of a conversation. We don't know whether a literal translation would be "*See you later*" or "*Your grandmother has nice teeth*," but we can observe whether the words have an emotional impact on either party. Likewise, the bird may not understand the moral implications of being good, but it will seek the acceptance being offered and can associate good things with the words being said.

Laughter, "*Good bird*," and "*Pretty bird*" are all examples of things that a grey will perceive as praise (reinforcement). Optimum results come when the words you choose are used with enthusiasm. If the bird does not pay attention when you say the words,

The leaves of common house plants are toxic and can kill a grey parrot, as can lead in the metal parts of artificial plants.

then the praise probably isn't getting through. The bird should at least make eye contact, possibly with only one eye. Preferably, the bird's eyes will pinpoint; it will move its head forward and slightly down, maybe cock its head to one side. A grey's head will be slightly "fluffy" so that the edges of the scalloped chest and neck feathers may take on a ruffled look. The bird might lift its foot to solicit being picked up. These are all indications of friendly intent and clues that the bird is accepting your praise and reinforcement. If the bird doesn't react, add enthusiasm, include games and "peek-a-boos," or increase volume until the bird responds.

When previously presented and adequately reinforced, praise can come before an action. Many times a bird will say *"Good bird"* just before performing appropriately. In this way, praise can represent a prompt. If you suspect the bird is considering misbehaving, particularly if there might be a reason to misbehave, such as to get your attention, you can say *"Good bird"* before the bird misbehaves. The bird may realize it has your attention so no further action is required, or it may be distracted long enough to change its mind.

Another word that can easily be established as a cue is *"Careful."* If a baby grey parrot is told at times when it might fall, or drop something, or lose footing to *"Be careful,"* the bird can learn that these words mean that something it doesn't want to happen might happen. If you can anticipate unwanted behavior, a well-patterned parrot can be influenced to avoid the unwanted behavior simply with the use of the words *"Be careful."*

Anticipate and Distract

Once cues are established, they can be used to distract from unwanted behavior. When we see a misbehavior coming—maybe a nip during step-ups—we can't just say *"No."* Many birds enjoy the drama of this exchange; others might perceive two opposite messages: *"Step-up!"* and *"No."* What's a bird to do?

We can say to the bird *"Are you going to be a good bird?"* Combined with eye contact, this technique can prevent misbehavior by reminding the bird not only of what is expected, but also of how it feels to enjoy the attention associated with the buzz words. It also reinforces the bird's sense that humans are in charge.

Anything that has been done once can be reinforced. Life is fun, and all creatures prefer to do things they enjoy. Since almost any nonviolent interaction with a human might be interpreted by the bird to be reinforcement, we must take care not to allow unwanted behaviors. For

Unnatural Behavior

Few things are more difficult than *not* saying *"No," "Don't,"* or *"Stop"* when a painfully sharp beak is closed or nearly closed around your finger. It's counterintuitive, and goes against the way most people would naturally respond, but changes in human/bird interactions must begin with us. If we can be trained to use words or body language more effectively to distract the bird, then bites can be eliminated. We can replace spontaneous unfamiliar behaviors with acceptable patterned ones. Familiar activities provide comfort to people and parrots alike. A well-patterned, well-reinforced interaction provides a sense of security to everyone involved because they know what will happen next.

example, if the bird is nipping in response to a particular set of interactions, you must redesign the way those interactions are performed. If the bird is nipping hands as it is coming off the cage, you might choose to temporarily step up the bird off the cage onto hand-held perches, or stop letting the bird stand on top of the cage. You might use the Good Hand/Bad Hand technique—distract the bird's eyes just before giving the step-up command—or perhaps have the bird step up onto towel-covered hands.

For accidental reinforcement of behavior, especially in a creature that is looking for any kind of attention (reward), as we have mentioned, even saying *"No"* can provide drama or excitement. A normal, creative parrot trained to anticipate praise (reward) for good behavior usually becomes more willing to seek new ways to generate rewards. The bird will also gradually abandon behaviors that do not bring at least occasional reinforcement. Reinforcement includes anything the bird enjoys. Verbal praise, a treat, a kiss on the beak, or a head scratch make very effective rewards.

Punishments and Quick Fixes

Especially because of the grey parrot's sensitive nature and well-developed fight-or-flight response, there is no such thing as an effective punishment. As a prey species, the bird's natural instinct to avoid danger must be respected. The effects of both punishments and reprimands are so counterproductive that even the mildest forms must be absolutely avoided. A nipping grey is not to be dropped, forcefully squirted, thumped on the beak, isolated in a scary place, or hit. Even if a reprimand temporarily or permanently causes the bird to discontinue the unwanted behavior, the potential for damaging the bird or the human/bird bond is very real. Additionally, even if a bird is not immediately affected by a reprimand,

damaging behavioral response—loss of trust—can appear later.

Distracting to appropriate behavior and positive reinforcement are the best means of modifying unwanted grey behavior. This is by far the easiest way to train a parrot. It is often successfully employed even though humans may be unaware of what they are doing. It's just as common for someone to accidentally reinforce good behaviors as it is to accidentally reinforce unwanted ones.

New, spontaneous changes may not become permanent change. Even step ups can be considered a "quick fix" if they are done only occasionally. The benefit of an immediate behavioral change can be the turning point in the attitudes of humans who create the bird's behavioral environment, even if it isn't automatically a permanent change. Human behavior can be difficult to change. Anything that can safely generate a one-time change can demonstrate what a companion bird is capable of and may be the best way to convince humans that if they change their ways, the bird's behavior will also change. Newly introduced changes are most likely to become habitual if they are reinforced during the first three to five days following their appearance. If changes are not almost immediately reinforced into patterns, the behavior will return to what it was before.

Biting

Parrots in the wild seldom bite each other. Biting appears in companion parrots as improvised behavior that has been reinforced into a habit. In addition to reinforcing the behavior with repetition, a person who is being repeatedly bitten during interactions with a grey parrot might be acting too confrontational and not inspirational enough. That is, humans must learn to appropriately encourage their companion parrots how to behave.

What to Do

Certainly, the best way to deal with biting is to prevent it, but if all efforts have failed and you are looking down at a grey parrot lacerating your flesh and unwilling to stop lacerating your flesh, what do you do?

If the bird is sitting on your hand, simply put it down. If it's sitting on a perch, it's pretty easy to get the bird to release by pushing the hand being bitten down toward the area just under the bird's beak; this creates an uncomfortable posture for the bird. Of course, this is absolutely counterintuitive. Most people experiencing a painful bite want to pull their hand away. If you pull away, you run the risk of ripping flesh, injuring the bird, or actually teaching

Anticipating and Preventing Bites

If a bird is learning to bite, it's time to shift gears—distract to other behavior—so that biting does not become habitual.

Most bites can be placed into one of three categories. If we first understand what stimulated the biting, it's easier to plan successful distractions.

1. Fear or anxiety biting is the first part of the fight-or-flight response.
- Be less confrontational.
- Improve access to feelings of safety.
- Don't force the bird out of the cage.
- Improve cooperation patterning using the towel game, eye games, or other nonthreatening strategies.
- Model cooperative behavior.

2. Territorial biting to defend a mate, status, toys, nest site, height, food, or water supply. This includes displaced aggression, which is biting something or someone the bird can reach out and bite when it cannot reach the individual it wants to bite.

- Watch for signs of territorial biting.
- Maintain eye contact.
- Put the bird down or handle it with hand-held perches or a towel.
- Increase cooperation exercises, handling, and outings to improve bonding.

3. Manipulation biting, learned behavior intended to get one's way, such as biting when the owner looks away, is on the phone, or is returning the bird to the cage.

- Avoid opportunities for the bird to engage in these behaviors, and therefore, to have these behaviors reinforced.
- Don't stop eye contact when answering the phone or returning the bird to the cage. Put the bird down before answering the phone. Behaviors that are not engaged in cannot be reinforced into habits.
- Again, continue handling with hand-held perches or with the towel game.
- Improve step-up and other forms of cooperation patterning.

the bird to bite by a response that will reinforce the behavior. Some birds will release if light-blocking fabric is placed over their heads. If the bird is hanging on and grinding, you might try introducing something else into the beak, deflecting the bird to bite down on a magazine or another object.

Eye contact is important here, for often, if you can catch the bird's eye, it will release the bite. A manufactured distraction may be necessary to change the determined bird's focus on the bite. That could mean clapping the other hand against your thigh or suddenly turning the television volume up with the remote.

Sound and Fury

A grey parrot's alarm calls can be ear piercing, annoying, enraging. Unwanted vocalizations in grey parrot homes involve a different type of sound than that encountered in most other parrot households. While they are not so loud as many other parrots' calls, they can be more painful to sensitive human ears, and if our observations are accurate, men have less tolerance for shrill sounds in the home than women.

In addition to possessing a few truly disturbing calls, greys have a natural attraction to sounds that fall within the natural range of their voices. A modern companion grey can do variations on all types of electronic tones: microwave, alarm clock, computer, oven timer, car

alarm, smoke detector, and tele-phone answering machine, among others. The most common noise complaint among grey parrots involves either natural alarm signals or learned electronic alarms as attention-demanding behavior.

Intrusive sounds can be artfully used by a grey parrot to intentionally annoy humans or merely to get their attention. These creative vocaliza-tions commonly occur when humans are in sight or within earshot, when they try to talk on the phone, talk to each other, leave the room, or watch television. It's no accident that copied tones are designed as alarms to stimulate humans to do some-thing—typically jump up and rush to the source of the sounds. Grey par-rots appear to find it quite amusing to be able to make humans jump up and run.

Of course, the best way to pre-vent attention-demanding noises in grey parrots is to ignore the behav-iors when they first appear. A behav-ior that is not reinforced usually disappears, but both signaling and "singing" can be self-rewarding. Beeps and whistles also seem to function as something resembling singing in some grey parrots. These birds will sing at regular times such as dinnertime and bright sunny mornings when others are singing and showering. These calls might be used in a sort of nervous way, when something isn't quite right, or they might be used to get attention. Birds that are using electronic tones as attention-demanding behaviors might scream out when the owner leaves the room, sits down, answers the phone, or tries to read, write, or work. Birds that are using these calls in a nervous way will settle down when necessary changes are made.

Of course, alarm calls and loud vocalizations are sometimes appropriate. If the bird's needs are not being met or if danger is present, the bird has every right to try to attract as much attention as necessary. If an otherwise quiet bird is making a fuss, investigate; maybe the water bowl is dry or dirty, or a cat, a mouse, or a fire is present. Sometimes, the bird is just trying to tell us something.

Obsenities

While the screaming parrot can be problematic for neighbors, frequent or untimely obscenities can adversely affect the quality of a bird's life by offending humans in its own home. Foul-mouthed birds may be increasingly isolated—perhaps banished to the garage or basement and banned from outings and social interactions with honored guests.

The most common nuisance word is usually an obscenity: "*Hot damn*" or "*Darn*" or more colorful expressions that most of us would not repeat in front of parents, clerics, children, or too-interested social workers. A parrot doesn't quite spontaneously invent words, although it can happen; the bird copies words it has heard.

So how did those particular words or sounds wind up coming out of this bird? The bird is mimicking something that stimulated an entertaining emotion in humans. Some people seem truly unaware that they have said the words that their birds are repeating. Mattie Sue has no clue why her macaw says "*Ouch*" every time she picks up a hammer.

Habitual behavior is created by at least two components: enactment (doing the behavior) and reinforcement (being rewarded for enacting the behavior). A new word will not be repeated frequently if the bird is not rewarded, usually with attention, for saying the word. Of course, some words can be self-rewarding.

The easiest way to get a bird to discontinue saying something is by

getting it to say or do something else. Try to determine what cues the bird to say the word. Divert the bird to a different word or behavior before the unwanted words or sounds are made. If the word or sound appeared only recently, often, simply ignoring the behavior will eliminate it.

Remodeling: Something I call "remodeling" is another valuable device that can be easily used to vanquish new nuisance words. If the bird is saying, for example, *"Damn it!"* we can often divert the pronunciation of the newly acquired word to something like *"Can it!"* This can be done either as a spontaneous response to the word or as a

Allowing a grey parrot on the shoulder can endanger a person who is not careful.

planned distraction before the use of the offensive word.

Remodeling can be combined with use of the model/rival method, which was often described by Dr. Irene Pepperberg in her work with Alex. This process involves setting up a competitive situation in which a human or other bird rival is rewarded for saying a more desirable word or pronunciation. If the bird says *"Damn it!"* and is not rewarded, and the rival bird or human assistant says *"Can it"* and is rewarded, then the bird, seeking to be rewarded, will learn to say *"Can it."*

If a behavior has been repeated for about 21 days, there is a good chance that it has become habitual; that is, it has become an established part of the bird's routine behavior. A bird that has been habitually repeating a nuisance phrase or sound for a few months or a few years will be a more difficult challenge than a bird that has only recently started repeating an expletive. A parrot will remember things it said years ago, just as you can remember how to say a word that you may not have spoken in many years, and just as you can remember how to play Monopoly and ride a bicycle, although you may not have done those things for quite some time. However, if there is sufficient reason not to say or do those old things from the past, humans and birds alike simply will not do or say them. How does this happen?

Behaviors that no longer serve a purpose become obsolete and are replaced by behaviors that have a

purpose in the current environment. Unused old behaviors are replaced by useful new behaviors, but changing any habitual behavior usually isn't easy.

In helping a bird to discontinue an established, habitual use of profanity, begin by evaluating when the profanity appears. Is it during play or during the regular practice of the bird's vocabulary? Does it occur at a particular time of day or when events in the home stimulate it as a response? If you know when a sound is usually made, you are well on your way to replacing that sound with a different one.

Burps, Belches, and Other Obnoxious Sounds

African greys are especially fond of making and observing reactions to coughing, burping, belching, and other sounds of bodily distress. Guiding a grey parrot away from these may be more difficult than guiding it away from profanity, as few spoken words resemble these sounds. Again, we must anticipate the behavior before it occurs and distract the bird to different behavior. The bird must be distracted to

It's amazing how many apartment managers who, when told that a potential resident has a parrot, know to ask, *"Does it bark?"*

Sounds acquired from other animals are among the most annoying vocalizations observed in grey parrots. Acquired animal sounds are, like human body sounds and electronic sounds, usually more difficult to modify than human words; however, they are also sometimes more predictably enacted at a particular time of day. A companion grey might do hen cockatiel at sunrise or Blue-crowned Amazon when it's time to eat.

To divert from these behaviors, the daily routine must be changed in some substantial way so that their enactment is avoided. The grey parrot that does hen cockatiel at sunrise might have to have a more lightproof cover so that it doesn't know when the sun rises. Then the breakfast routine can be changed in some way to create an entirely different interactive ritual, perhaps by removing the bird to a perch to eat breakfast rather than providing the morning meal in the cage.

sounds that are both more acceptable to humans and achieve just as entertaining a reward for the bird. Laughing at a bird that sounds like it's farting reinforces the behavior. With reactions like laughter, horror, disgust, etc., making these sounds and watching for reactions is a type of self-rewarding activity. It's usually easy to distract an interested, well-motivated bird to laughter before the gross body sounds begin. Again, if you've been unable to divert it away from an unwanted sound, be sure not to laugh after it begins.

Lack of Stimulation

Like a person with an addictive personality, a grey parrot that finds joy in only one or two activities is likely to become obsessed with those few things. This is one more example of how lack of stimulation creates unwanted behavior in companion birds. That famous old source of almost all bird behavioral issues, boredom, also contributes to habitually redundant behaviors including the repeating of nuisance words and sounds.

Here we can expand the bird's experiences so that it learns new ways to enjoy life. If the bird is encouraged to do many different, diverse behaviors, nuisance sounds will gradually disappear.

Progressive Fearfulness

An individual grey's personality is a combination of learned and inherited characteristics. In captivity, the bird has no predators, but rather, may exhibit an inherited tendency to respond with fear to many situations. Even boredom can lead to induced or enhanced fear reactions in a grey parrot. Accidental reinforcement can cause cautiousness to progress to shyness, fearfulness, panic, or even phobic behaviors.

Both caution and true fear are important in the life of any wild bird. Greys can be seen circling a clearing before they land as they are prey species that must be always watchful for those who would make dinner of them. Because of how easily most African parrots turn to the fight-or-flight response, it's easy to surmise that these birds are probably more subject to predation in the wild than their New World or Pacific species relatives.

In captivity, fear response contributes to behavioral problems such as biting—the "fight" part of a well-developed fight-or-flight response—thrashing, falling, inability to regrow repeatedly knocked-out wing feathers, and even (commonly) feather shredding or snapping or (rarely) feather plucking. Shyness, fearfulness, and phobic behavior rather than aggression often accompany self-induced feather damage—shredding, snapping, or plucking—in companion grey parrots.

Within the African grey parrots, the Timneh appears to be more resistant to the development of truly phobic responses than Red-tailed greys. A domestic-raised companion Timneh is rarely as easily provoked

to the fight-or-flight response as a companion Red-tailed grey. However, fear-biting and thrashing can be seen in both species.

Repeated enactment of the fight-or-flight response by a grey parrot, or sometimes even one severe incidence of the fight-or-flight response induced by panic, can stimulate ongoing, constant panic behaviors whenever humans are present. We have likened this condition to phobic mental illness, but we are not altogether sure that this condition doesn't serve some unknown purpose. Sometimes, despite the best intentions, the hardest work, and the kindest handling, a grey parrot inexplicably falls into this behavior. If this behavior were com-

pletely maladaptive, we believe it would not appear in these birds. There must be some adaptive aspect for the wild grey. "Under normal circumstances stress responses are beneficial and permit the animal to react more competently to an emergency. However, when the stressful challenge is prolonged, the responses become maladaptive, leading to decreased resistance to disease and abnormal behavior."

Cautiousness

Although wild greys are cautious by nature, in the home, cautiousness can be seen as a tendency toward shyness or developing fearfulness. While a fear response can be direct and immediate, a grey parrot doesn't always respond immediately to a situation. The grey likes to sit back and assess a situation, often drawing clues from others—humans, birds, and so on—to determine the appropriate reaction. New toys and new people may have to wait through an assessment period, which varies in length depending on the bird, before the parrot is ready for interaction.

Panic

After assessing a situation, the grey might decide it is scary and respond with fear. The most extreme form of fear is panic, which involves growling and thrashing. Humans who are watching the bird with wide eyes to see how it will respond are exhibiting body language that signals caution or fear to the bird; however, some greys that know their owners might understand that this isn't really what the human means. Many greys see their human as having the cautious pose a grey would take if it perceived danger. No matter how the bird reaches the decision, fear is a response to an object or situation that has been determined to be a threat.

When a grey's fear is generalized and the bird panics in many situations, it is sometimes labeled phobic. A phobic bird exhibits unreasonable fear. It will broadly generalize what situations should be feared, so that humans may no longer be able to identify exactly what the bird fears.

It's not unusual for greys to fear hands or eyes. Manipulating a parrot's perception of appearance, such as by hiding hands or by allowing the bird to see only one eye at a time, as it would see another bird, can sometimes generate more appropriate responses. Diet can also contribute to hypersensitivity similar to phobic behaviors.

Maturing

African greys are helpless when they hatch and must depend upon their parents—natural or human—to supply every need in order to survive. During the months parents have control, a young grey parrot must be given all the information required to live on its own. At a certain point, the bird must be ready to become physically and emotionally independent.

When a grey reaches the state where it should become independent and is either lacking the tools to function independently or perceives that a human or humans have too much control, the parrot experiences stress. At this point the bird should be able to make food choices and meet its own nutritional needs. It should be able to climb and hold onto perches. Nails should have points sharp enough to grip, and perches shouldn't be too large in diameter. The bird's wings must be long enough to control falls. The bird must be able to entertain itself when nobody else is around. It must be able to call to "flock members" and to feel like part of a flock. Problematic fear responses may appear when the bird is forced to be independent before it is ready or when it is not given enough independence when it is ready.

A hand-fed grey's experiences with its surrogate human parents affect its view of relationships with people. The "parent" is trusted to help the baby parrot learn the tools needed to function. If the job is handed off to another person, the bird's sense of security can be seriously undermined. Weaning the baby onto solid food in preparation for life in captivity is best completed by the same parent or set of parents.

Balance and Grip

Improper grooming, especially improperly trimmed wing feathers, can contribute to fearfulness in African grey parrots. A parrot uses

crashing into the window or from gaining enough speed to injure itself. The bird should be nearly able to fly. Secondary feathers should never be cut since these are the feathers that provide control in landing. Like the inside flaps on an airplane's wings, the secondary flight feathers are the "brakes," and a bird cannot stop gracefully and confidently without them. There should always be enough of the primary feathers left to protect the growth of new primary feathers.

Blood feathers on a grey are very sensitive, especially on the wings, particularly if the feathers are over-trimmed. A bird with new primaries growing in may become very protective of its wings. It might avoid flapping and any situations that might stimulate flapping. If a bird is feeling especially protective of its wings, if it senses any "danger," it might resist coming out of the cage. Many parrot owners, having been bullied by other types of parrots by not taking enough control, will try to force the bird to come out of the cage, whether it wants to or not. A grey might balk at having the issue pushed. A typical scenario is that the bird falls to the bottom of the cage, breaking the feather it was protecting. Now the bird is holding a grudge against the owner for causing the fall so that it might panic and automatically jump or thrash the next time it sees the owner, and a cycle of fearfulness begins.

The grey parrot's sensitive temperament is best served with very

its wings, toenails, and beak in basic locomotion. If any of these are rendered useless, the bird is in danger of falling. Uncontrolled falling can establish fear of falling. This leads the bird to fear climbing and to fear stepping onto surfaces, such as a hand, that might then be fallen from. Since the only escape mechanism has been removed, the bird might actually become afraid of being afraid. This is when true phobia sets in, and the bird will begin to panic in more and more circumstances. Eventually almost anything sends the bird thrashing and growling to the floor of the cage.

A young grey's wings should be trimmed only enough to keep it from

noninvasive grooming configuration and technique. Consider the possibility that a bird outgrowing a fearful phase might regain self-assurance exactly as those old, cut wing feathers are replaced with full new ones. A grey parrot with a tendency to be overly cautious may require full wing feathers in order to retain confidence. Both phobic behaviors and feather-damaging disorders of all types are probably more common in grey parrots with trimmed wing feathers. These individuals should be allowed to keep full wings.

The Red-tailed grey and, to a lesser extent, the Timneh can have a tendency to knock new wing feathers out as they regrow. If a bird is having trouble regrowing wing feathers, be sure to provide smaller than usual, easily gripped perches to prevent falling and thrashing. Limit the number of toys, but provide multiple chewable branches on which to climb and exercise both wings and beaks. Sometimes trimming off the open part of the feather as the new feather is growing in will make the feather less likely to be knocked out, but be sure not to cut into the membrane providing blood supply.

Messages from Humans

Sometimes, the stimulus for a bird's panic response comes from human caregivers. If a bird has developed a fear of fast-moving hands, or if hands change in appearance, such as with a bright, new manicure, the bird might respond with mistrust or outright fear. If this happens, try holding hands out of sight—in pockets or behind your back until calm interaction can be stimulated, patterned, and reinforced. Also, expect reactions to changes in hair color, haircut, or hats.

A grey parrot that has reacted negatively might thrash, bite, or flee any human eye contact. This can be distressing when feeding or cleaning the cage. If it is possible without provoking the bird, remove a grey parrot when servicing the cage. Try avoiding eye contact if you must service the cage with the bird inside. A bird can be slowly guided out of this behavior by use of games and non-threatening interactions.

Eyes

A grey parrot's eyes are almond-shaped or almost squinty when it is calm and relaxed, while a human has a tendency to round the eyes when feeling compassionate or concerned. A grey can translate this as nervousness or fear and it may become afraid as well. This may happen when a person is introducing something new to a grey or is being introduced to a new grey. You can more effectively convey calmness and confidence to a grey by slightly squinting your eyes. It's even better to include moving the head forward and slightly lower to mimic the grey.

Basic Guide to Easy Games

Some grey parrots simply prefer to interact in ways not involving contact. This might include, but is not limited to, dancing, singing, eye games, peek-a-boos, fetch, and other nontactile interactions. Especially with shy birds, it's a real advantage to know how to play without touching.

1. If a bird reacts fearfully to hands and eyes, hide your hands and look at a cautious or unfamiliar bird with one eye at a time. This eye should be squinting and not wide open.

2. If eye contacting is threatening, don't maintain eye contact. Squint your eyes until nearly shut. Gradually open them as the bird becomes comfortable looking at you and letting you look back.

3. Remain motionless until the bird moves. A grey parrot might remain absolutely motionless when confronted with a stranger. If you copy this behavior, the bird is likely to recognize you as behaviorally similar, and therefore, probably a safe flock member.

4. Stoop over so that your entire head is lower than the bird's body. Because of the desire to achieve the highest status in the flock, many birds naturally gain confidence by being higher than humans. Almost any parrot finds people sitting on the floor absolutely baffling and will often come down to see what they are doing there.

5. Play blink. A frightened animal won't blink while maintaining eye contact. Demonstrate that you are unafraid by blinking during eye contact. An interested, interactive parrot will close its eyes or blink back to show that it does not fear you either.

6. Play peek-a-boo around any interesting corner, reading materials, towels, or clothing—not your hands, as a shy grey parrot may be sensitive to hands.

7. Mimic the bird's friendly body language. When the bird stretches a greeting by extending one or both wings (mantling), demonstrate that you feel the same way by exhibiting the same behavior.

8. Mimic simple sounds from across the room or around a corner including tapping or knocking when you hear the bird tap or knock. If the bird rings a bell, try ringing a bell in response. Try to entice the bird to respond to your response.

9. Share food. If the bird is cautious and has never taken food from your hand, it might avoid it, throw the food, or drop it. The bird might be persuaded to take the food by manipulating the window of opportunity during which the food is offered. This is also called "Keep Away." Offer the food, then drop it or take it away. Wait a few seconds, then offer the food again, dropping it or taking it away before the bird can accept it. Also, giving the food to a rival increases the effectiveness of this game.

10. Play fetch. This is probably the game most frequently initiated by parrots with humans: the bird drops the toy or spoon or grape; the human picks it up and hands it to the bird. The bird flashes its eyes, takes the toy, then suddenly drops it again. The human picks it up, etc.

11. "I'll wear toys for you." Arrange to have old glasses, small wooden or plastic toys, or bird-safe jewelry that the bird can steal. Play with toys or have someone else play with them and allow the bird to steal or compete for the toys.

12. Demonstrate the pleasure of touching with other humans, pets, or birds. Find a cooperative friend who enjoys being hugged and touched and petted and demonstrate the joys of hugging, touching, and petting the bird. This game resembles the model/rival method of speech training in that it can stimulate competition. It can teach your bird good behavior.

One-on-One

Sometimes a bird going through a fearful stage meets a human to whom it is naturally, inexorably drawn. Like a thunderbolt, this is love at first sight. Curiously, in greys, this is not always a situation of "overbonding," in which, after falling for a particular human, the bird remains fearful or aggressive with other humans. Grey parrots that were previously panicked by interactions with any human may learn to accept humans after meeting only one human with whom it naturally connects.

Sometimes a bird encounters a person it sees as a rival or a threat, or it will suddenly decide that it is terrified of someone who has done nothing to deserve such treatment. The bird can be gently guided away from these feelings. Start with games and nonthreatening, nontactile interactions. Use the disfavored person's name in tandem with the bird's: "Jaco's Uncle Charlie" or "Uncle Charlie's Jaco" when guiding the bird to include the person in its group of accepted associates, then progress to the towel game, step-ups, and outings with this persona non grata.

Greys do not like to change their minds and pushing them to do so is often rewarded with resentment. An insecure grey may actually use hating someone as a way to build confidence. A grey parrot might discontinue negative reactions to a person when that negative behavior no longer serves a purpose. Waiting for the bird to change its mind is sometimes the best recourse.

Whistling

As mentioned, greys like to whistle and can often be persuaded to strike up a relationship with anyone willing to participate. Whistling can distract from being fearful and can provide a sense of communicating with the flock. This interaction can foster a sense of security and should be included in daily interactions, whether the bird is fearful or not.

Outings

Sometimes just taking the bird for a ride in the car can generate noticeable improvement in relationships. The bird might feel better connected to a less-favored person in unfamiliar locations or situations. Improved bonding can result, especially if there is an opportunity for a true rescue scenario.

Professional Intervention

The grey parrot's extreme intelligence renders it more behaviorally sensitive than many other parrots. A grey can easily learn or improvise a very impressive array of diverse unwanted behaviors. If humans are repeatedly outsmarted by a cantankerous grey or baffled by a totally terrified bird, professional intervention

Social Rescue

Better bonds can be forged between a parrot and a human it doesn't like through mutual adventures. It probably works something like this:

Did you ever walk into a social gathering and know absolutely no one in the room, and then, after an hour of lingering by the punch bowl, feeling awkward and out of place, you see an acquaintance across the room. Maybe it's someone you didn't particularly like before or have been lukewarm to at best. In unfamiliar surroundings, suddenly, that person looks really safe and familiar and reminds you of home.

Then, out of nowhere, comes the most annoying stranger you've ever seen, walking straight up to you and putting a hand on your forearm. You withdraw and turn to go, but the annoying person follows you through the crowd. Suddenly, your acquaintance, the one you didn't like before, steps between you and the awful stranger.

"Back off," that now-lovely person says to the awful stranger, taking your arm and leading you to a quiet foyer.

A better bond is forged. That relationship is changed forever. The new bond will be even stronger in a potentially dangerous setting.

In the same way, if a less-favored person is the only familiar person in a strange place, the bird will be very nice to that person at that time in that location. This sets up a pattern for the bird to also be nice in other places at other times. This works especially well if it can involve a rescue scenario, as in Androcles and the Lion.

might make a huge difference. A bird that cannot be touched may prove perfectly cooperative with a professional stranger. Owners might not even recognize that precious creature with just a tiny remnant of yesterday's blood on the tip of its beak.

If you need help, seek a parrot behavior consultant who can document experience with grey parrots. Professionals in this relatively new field can be the first line of defense against the accumulation of troubling issues. Potential problems that might require professional assistance include: fearfulness, biting, diving, behavioral feather chewing, and annoying vocalizations.

An effective behavioral counselor probably works more like a golf or tennis coach than a psychiatrist. A behavioral consultant should be more focused on how to change the bird's behavior than on judging how it evolved. A good behaviorist deals compassionately with the bird and with the owner. Most behaviorists probably prefer an in-home consultation and will probably take a history in order to plan strategies for changing the bird's behavior.

Your favorite breeder, bird store, or avian veterinarian should be able to refer you to a reputable parrot behavior consultant in your area. If no such professional is available they might recommend telephone counseling. Quite a few counseling alternatives are available in the consultant ads in your favorite bird magazine and on the Internet. Some are wonderful; some might make matters worse. Look for places where kindness and open minds prevail. Ask for references from those who have actually worked with a particular consultant about a similar problem in a grey parrot and expect:

- an initial screening evaluation by telephone including an evaluation of your responses; to be referred to a different consultant if either of you don't feel connected
- an offer of group, telephone, or in-home counseling
- an analysis of diet, housing, and handling
- grooming or toweling the bird in order to observe its responses
- an evaluation of feather condition and the bird's responses to showering
- possible veterinarian referral
- confidentiality unless you give permission to write about the case, which can be done in a way to protect your privacy
- to be offered more than one option for the modification the problem

A behavior consultant might not even touch a shy bird, as invasive handling can worsen such conditions. In cases involving shyness or fearfulness, expect to be offered suggestions regarding adjusting the environment rather than handling. This may be the easiest, most obvious, and most effective way to change bird behavior. Some environmental manipulations might worsen or reinforce the unwanted behaviors, so sometimes the environmental elements are manipulated in various ways to study the bird's responses.

What Else to Expect

Expect the behavior consultant to seem to be favoring the welfare of the bird over human interests. As an advocate for the bird, a responsible consultant must be ever-vigilant, as many subtle human interactions may prove dangerous to a bird. Whether a situation involves other pets, rambunctious children, spousal abuse, drug or alcohol abuse, or simply danger from Teflon cookware and excessive forgetfulness, a caring consultant will try to confront the problem, sometimes by referring to human behavioral and psychological counseling. The relationship between the family and the consultant should be friendly and interactive.

Every bird and every environment is different, and you are the most significant element of the bird's environment. Some humans can more readily understand and implement one type of plan than another; therefore, any bird behavior consultant worth his or her salt should be able to suggest more than one approach to the modification of a particular behavior. An effective communicator should be able to explain the same approach in more than one way so that all parties—even young children—can understand and implement a behavioral intervention program.

Expect to participate in the process by stimulating and reinforcing appropriate new behaviors, for only by training humans will enduring changes be produced in the bird.

Expect to see new behaviors. Whenever an old behavior disappears, new ones arise. These may be transitional rather than permanent changes. Be prepared to make further changes.

It is important to like and to trust the professionals who work with your bird; your life and your bird's life may be changed from this day on. Expect to enjoy the interaction and to have your life touched in a significant way. It's not unusual to weep with joy when a major breakthrough is seen.

Nobody—not even a bird—exactly forgets a behavior. Old behaviors are replaced with new ones. In addition, behavior doesn't immediately change permanently. That is, it comes and goes. A behavior doesn't suddenly stop. It stops, then reappears, then stops, then reappears, swinging back and forth like a pendulum. If behavioral intervention is working, each reappearance of unwanted behavior

will be of shorter duration and less intensity. There will be more tail wags and other happiness behaviors, more enactments of behaviors being reinforced, and the incidents of unwanted behavior will slowly disappear.

Dreaming of Paradise

The environment might provide a sense of security or destroy it. A feeling of constant danger can harm a bird's health and disposition. Noisy species such as large cockatoos or macaws may upset shyer birds that perceive that loud, frequent vocalizations indicate the presence of danger. We might address this issue by housing species separately, or we

may be able to build in a sense of safety with other environmental elements. Manipulating height, housing the bird either higher or lower, for example, can enhance a sense of security, as can the addition of hiding opportunities, perhaps a little tent (hide box), a towel over part of the cage, restricted sight of other birds, or moving the cage to a more sheltered location across the room from traffic areas.

Reroofing, remodeling, or loud construction nearby can absolutely destroy an established grey's sense of safety. A parrot expressing stress reactions to any temporary situation might benefit from being boarded or simply staying with Aunt Lucy for the duration of the problem.

Everything comes down to the necessity that everyone's needs—parrots' and people's—are met. While we can try to provide as full a life as possible, it is not to our benefit, or that of the birds, to believe that everything necessary for a quality life has been furnished. When we delude ourselves into thinking that we have done everything fully and completely, we may be overlooking opportunities to learn new ways to make life better for ourselves and our feathered friends.

Chapter Twelve
All About Feathers

Few parrot care issues are more complex and confounding, especially to the owners of afflicted grey parrots, than feather destructive behavior. Even professionals with a history of successfully helping naked parrots regrow feathers may have little or no proof that one thing or another caused a particular incident. Sometimes a cure is miraculously accessible, even if the source is unknown. Sometimes the source is obvious, but a cure cannot be accessed. Especially with this disorder, which is almost exclusive to companion birds, cause is less important than recovery. Only today counts. Even the most stable companion parrot might be tearing out feathers tomorrow.

Field biologist David Manry tells us that a wild animal confronted with a situation it does not have a corresponding instinctual behavior for may substitute another behavior rather than doing nothing at all. The animal can become obsessive about this inappropriate behavior and perform it to extremes. Almost anything in the animal's repertoire can be used as a "displacement behavior" including preening, pulling, or even chewing feathers, nails, or skin.

Companion African grey parrots often must confront situations for which they have absolutely no instinctual response. Without our help, guidance, research, planning, and sometimes hard work they can wind up naked.

Molting and Other Explainable Feather Loss

Some new bird owners may be concerned that their baby greys are "secretly plucking feathers" because feathers are found on the floor or cage bottom. This is a common summer complaint, and there is usually little cause for concern as this is simply a part of molting, the natural process of the cycle in which feathers replace themselves. Every year, a grey parrot loses and regrows feathers in a symmetrical configuration along the lines of circulation known as feather tracts. Most obviously, wing and tail feathers are molted and grow in mirror image, a configuration that doesn't affect flight ability. If a companion grey's wing or tail feathers are not growing

in the sleeping area. Try to head these self-injuries off before they occur, as feather follicles might suffer permanent damage and feathers that are repeatedly knocked out might not regrow. Knocked out wing feathers are a special cause for concern, for these are intended to stay in place and function to help the bird escape even under the most arduous circumstances, while tail feathers are loosely connected and might be left behind if quick escape is necessary. A sudden hot spell can result in the loss of multiple tail feathers, while missing wing feathers may go virtually unnoticed because of the symmetrical way they are replaced.

Chewing, Shredding, or Fringing

The most common form of feather destructive behavior in greys begins with damage to the outside edge of feathers—the barbs and barbules—resulting in a notched, fringed, or hairlike appearance. These behaviors may be transitional or progressive and can sometimes exist for years before anyone notices. The first sign of this type of feather damage is often visible as individual "fibers" or remnants of the barbs seen floating on the surface of the water dish, floating in the air, or clinging to the television screen. This form of feather damage can begin with "overpreening" during dry

in symmetrically, this could be an indication of follicle damage, or an environmental or behavioral issue.

Feather loss or damage can also be caused by other birds. If places that the bird itself cannot reach— cheeks, head, or nape—are being damaged, then the source is obviously another parrot. If you want the bird to have feathers on those spots, then the birds should be separated.

Night Frights

Sensitive greys may even experience something similar to "night frights" so common in cockatiels. Look for mice or other disturbances

winter months. If the bird has not learned independent toy play and seeks constant face-to-face interction with people, it might simply sit around preening when no human companion is available.

Feather Snapping

Feather snapping, a more acute, quickly progressing form of feather damage, is not uncommon in grey parrots. Snapping involves breaking the shaft of the feather. This can begin in a small way when a bird snaps off the *rachis* or central feather shaft near the outer end of the feather resulting in feathers ending in a V shape. In a more acute phase, this might involve snapping feathers off at the base, leaving no contour feather visible outside the down. The bird might snip the con-

tour feather and down feathers off, leaving bare patches of skin showing. Wing and tail feathers are typically targeted for this type of damage. This form of feather damage can appear suddenly. A bird might be in full feather when you leave for work in the morning, but you might come home in the afternoon to a naked bird with a pile of feathers under the perch. Feather snapping does not injure the skin, and there is no danger of skin infection as when a feather is pulled from

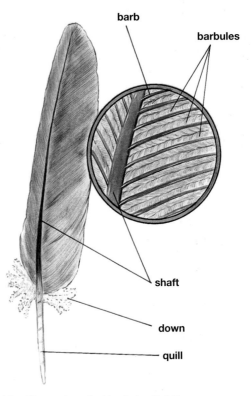

Tiny filaments called barbules link the barbs that come off the central feather shaft or rachis.

Active juveniles often damage tail feathers during play and may not retain a full, beautiful tail until about two years of age.

beak or feet. A parrot might target fully formed feathers or immature feathers retaining blood supply. These behaviors can pose a risk for skin infections.

Feather pulling is especially common around the vent or around the uropygial (preening) gland, as well as around the neck or over the crop where dirty feathers might be especially annoying to the bird. Pulling or chewing off dirty feathers is common behavior in baby parrots that have not yet experienced their first molt. It might be ongoing, or it might be a simple temporary response to dirty or damaged feathers.

Addressing this issue should begin with a trip to the veterinarian. If no health issues are present, occasional feather pulling, especially by juveniles, often resolves spontaneously with the molt, and is no cause for concern. However, a juvenile pulling, snapping, or chewing off dirty or damaged feathers should be bathed more often, exercised more, monitored carefully, and special care should be taken not to reinforce the behavior.

Ongoing feather pulling in adult greys, more than any other form of self-inflicted feather damage, is suspected to have an organic origin. If there is no identifiable illness, we must suspect food, fumes, or allergies when this behavior appears.

the follicle, but a bird can't recover from it until it molts; as feather shafts remain in the follicles, new feathers can't come in until these old shafts fall out.

Feather Plucking or Pulling

True feather plucking involves pulling the entire feather out of the follicle. Any feather can be targeted. The bird might pull feathers with the

Where and When

The most common places for grey parrots to begin damaging feathers are the upper legs or thighs, feathers around the neck in a necklace pattern, the sides of the chest just over the thighs, the tops of the wings going down the back, or in the shallow depressions on the back under the wings. This will be evident by the appearance of patches of damaged feathers, patches of gray down poking out through the smooth contour feathers, or actual bald spots. Birds chewing on new feathers will often leave feather particles in the water dish, and bald spots may be slow to appear. Greys will sometimes snap off wing feathers. This might seem like normal molting of the flight feathers unless the owner carefully inspects them to make sure the follicle end of the feather is present.

Maybe artificially heated dry air is to blame. Maybe it's holiday stress, but the most common time for feather picking to appear in African greys is November through February. Whether this is a result of seasonal hormonal cycles, indoor winter air quality, lack of humidity, or a response to artificial light or heat is unknown, but each of these elements might play a part.

Stress Reactions

Because self-induced feather damage is considered to be a reaction to stress, you must look, first of all, when this syndrome appears, for illness or physical problems. See an avian veterinarian at the first sign of unexplainable feather damage. Don't wait; go quickly, before the behavior becomes habitual. It's all right to ask about potential illness, zinc and calcium levels, yeast, and giardia. Be prepared to hear your local veterinarian's experience with contributing health-related issues in your specific geographic area. Sometimes, the veterinarian will find no health-related issues and will suggest diet or habitat manipulation and/or professional behavior counseling.

Self-mutilation

While feather damage is often mild and not an outright threat to the bird's health, self-inflicted damage to skin requires immediate medical and professional behavioral intervention. The self-destruction of skin, the skin on the feet, or even toes can be related to inappropriate perches, poor diet, or to inhaled environmental toxins, including nicotine.

Most behavior consultants probably agree that skin damage is probably more related to physiological sources than behavioral ones, although it might begin with something physically wrong and continue as a habit even after the medical issue is resolved.

Certain disease states are notorious for bringing on bouts of feather-damaging behavior. For this reason, the first step in combating such an incident is a complete veterinary workup. Disease states in parrots are generally a reflection of stress that may be physical or emotional, real or imagined. So, while the veterinarian may find a physical cause related to the self-destructive behavior, presumably this is not the sole cause of the problem, as the disease itself may be stress-related. When possible, it is preferable that a holistic approach be taken with self-mutilating birds. There is almost always much more to treat than a disease.

Aspergilosis, giardia, and staph infections are commonly associated with feather picking. These are generally considered "opportunistic" organisms, invading a body whose immune system is impaired or otherwise compromised. Thyroid conditions may also be commonly diagnosed. Thyroid malfunction is difficult to diagnose positively, and treating minor thyroid problems medically can increase the bird's stress and exacerbate damage rather then reduce it.

Health problems must be eradicated before fully focusing on emotional issues. In many places where there are no veterinarians available who have experience with birds, doctors may be worried about missing a medical condition and therefore will prescribe medication "just in case." While their intentions are good and this treatment plan might work under other circumstances, feather pickers should not be treated in this manner. The simple act of treating them can increase stress, making the problem worse, and there is always a risk that medication can harm or inhibit normal body functions.

Drugs: Some veterinarians may wish to treat self-induced feather damage with such drugs as Valium, Haldoperidol, or Prozac. Although medical treatment is absolutely necessary when illness or other uncomfortable health conditions exist, benefits from the use of tranquilizers or other mood enhancers are, as yet, unproven. These treatments should be considered temporary, last resort prescriptions used only after all efforts have been made to resolve the problem with behavioral or environmental techniques.

Holistic approaches: Holistic approaches can often correct problems less invasively and address some other contributing aspects. Contact allergies can be implicated in many cases of plucking associated with the legs in particular. Smokers carry elements of tobacco on their fingers. Some birds can be sensitive to certain types of wood used in perches or to the bacteria that can grow on them. Parrots can be sensitive to foods or to the artificial ingredients some foods contain. Artificial colors and preservatives are best avoided. Parrots can also have allergies to airborne particles and suffer something akin to hay fever in humans.

Dry Skin or External Parasites?

Some greys might pick at themselves in a manner suggesting a sudden extreme itch or bug crawling on them. To the human eye, the bird's skin might appear dry and flaky. It's tempting to think that the bird has dry skin or mites and to want to spray it with something to solve the problem, but again, this is not usually a situation to treat. Parrot skin often has a dry appearance to it, and in many of the places where parrots are kept as pets, there are no mites around that could infect the bird.

Healthy skin is also a result of proper diet. Humans might treat their own dry skin with lotions, but dry skin in humans comes from subjecting the skin to harsh chemicals and sun, improper diet, dehydration, and excessive salt, caffeine, or alcohol. Parrots, hopefully, do not have these problems. If a grey's skin is actually dry, the source must be identified rather than trying to treat it topically. A rain forest bird that now lives in the desert may need a humidifier and frequent showers to keep the skin sufficiently hydrated.

Diet, Exercise, and Showers

Like humans, parrots have a better attitude and outlook when they have been eating well. A poor or inadequate diet stresses not only the body, but the psyche as well. Fresh foods are very important in a bird's diet. A variety of organic produce would be most desirable as birds can react to coatings and pesticides.

The mixes suggested by Alicia McWatters, Ph.D., or in *Psittacine Aviculture* by Richard Schubott, are excellent bases for a balanced diet of fresh foods.

Greys may be less finicky when fed pellets and fresh food instead of seed as the base diet. Pellets are also the easiest way for most bird keepers to provide a nutritious diet. Preferably, pellets should contain few or no preservatives or artificial colors and a large number of food ingredients. Water should be clean and clear without vitamins or other additives. Anything added to the water can accumulate on the beak and can be deposited on the feathers while preening. Some parrots develop feather-picking habits because they do not have access to clean water.

Food sensitivities might be contributing to feather pulling, so manipulation of the bird's diet can help. Sometimes eliminating salt or oil and, in African greys more than other parrots, improving calcium sources and absorption can sometimes help. Occasionally, radical evaluation of the diet must be made, possibly removing all but one food from the diet and then gradually adding foods to observe their effect on the bird.

The entire makeup of an African grey, every bone and metabolic process, lends itself to explosive expenditures of energy. This is not an exclusively metabolic and physical process, but rather, also fills emotional needs. Few of our captive feathered friends are getting the exercise they really need. This has repercussions on their overall physical health, attitude, and stress levels.

Flapping: Placing the bird on a play area does no more to ensure adequate exercise than dropping a devoted couch potato off at the gym. Both will probably spend most of the time standing around. Humans must encourage the bird to work off excess energy by flapping exercises, which are best done over a bed or soft carpeted floor in case the bird should fall. Lowering the hand the bird is standing on or rolling it back and forth can encourage the bird to flap. A hand-held perch can be slowly rolled in the same manner. A grey parrot needs to flap every day

until it is breathing deeply, probably with its beak open.

Showering: Likewise, regular showering can resolve several stresses associated with feather mutilation, such as lack of adequate humidity and soiled feathers. Showering uses excess energy that can turn into frustration and is refreshing to the bird. A showered bird also uses its preening energy more evenly over its whole body. An unshowered bird would be more likely to preen problem spots such as the sides of the chest or over the back, leading to ragged and over-preened feathers.

Spraying: Parrots have taste buds on the roof of the mouth and no saliva on their tongues. Spraying a bad-tasting substance on feathers usually has no effect. Many times, the substance sprayed will be viewed as dirt, and the parrot will preen even harder. Occasionally, a bird will stop picking if the owner is diligent about spraying the bitter substance; however, parrots usually have the same good results with clear, clean water.

The Cage

The cage should be designed in a manner useful to the bird and placed in an appropriate location. Some birds prefer to be able to see what is going on while still being out of the way of actual action. It is rarely a good idea to put a feather picker out of the way where no one will bother it as this may increase anxiety related to separation from the flock. Raising or lowering the cage will almost always affect the grey's sense of security, some doing better when lowered, others preferring to be higher. Some birds stop picking feathers when relocated to a smaller, more secure cage. Others will start picking if they feel trapped or too confined in a small cage.

Lighting, Sleep, and Entertainment

There are three types of cones or light-detecting cells in our eyes. These structures provide us with visual interpretation of color. One type of cone detects blue light, one red, and one green. Birds have four types of cones for visual interpretation of color, and the wavelengths of light they are sensitive to are shifted to the left of the spectrum. They do not pick up as much information from the red end of the spectrum as we do, however; they pick up more information from the violet and ultraviolet ends of the spectrum. Since we cannot see it, we have no idea what things reflect light in this end of the spectrum.

Full-Spectrum Lighting

Lighting that is labeled "full-spectrum" may be a full-spectrum light as perceived by humans, or may be a full-spectrum light as perceived by birds. A full-spectrum light serving birds would emit wavelengths in the part of the spectrum parrots can appreciate, which means more toward the UV. The manufacturer should provide this information.

Keeping a bird under lighting with a limited visual spectrum limits the colors the bird can see. This might be similar to a human trying to live under only "black light." While we could learn to function, some of us would be extremely stressed by the situation. Some individuals might seem fine, although they haven't experienced the light of day in decades. Others experience amazing health improvements when provided full-spectrum lighting, which might include actual sunlight. Many greys have regrown feathers after the addition of this one crucial element.

Adequate Sleep

Adequate, continuous, nighttime sleep is a very effective stress reducer. African greys are from equatorial regions of Africa where there is little seasonal change in day length. These parrots need 10 to 12 hours of sleep at night year-round. Daytime naps do not make up for lost sleep at night. Sometimes this means making use of a sleep cage, a small cage in a separate room, so the bird is not disturbed by late-night television or visitors

Boredom

Boredom is a major contributor to feather mutilating. Life in captivity is never going to be as exciting as life in the wild, and we probably don't want it to be. Giving the bird appropriate toys and encouraging it to make use of them is one of the fun challenges the bird owner faces. The human's creativity needs to match the bird's and this is often harder than it sounds.

Much of the stress in a parrot's life can come from feelings of being isolated from the flock. In the wild, parrots continually connect vocally with each other. These vocalizations are a source of security and entertainment. If humans, at least occasionally, respond to a bird's calls, then the bird will feel much more content. Playing vocal games back and forth by either singing or whistling and matching each others' notes can combat boredom. Repeating words by labeling actions and objects can lend predictability to the parrot's life. Often, the bird will learn the words associated with the objects or actions and be able to indicate desires or needs, thereby increasing the bird's control over its life.

Sitting alone all day can be boring. No matter how many toys are in the cage or what radio station you leave playing, these are still very social animals. Parrots are very flexible in that they will welcome almost any creature as part of the flock. A cat or dog or canary or even a fish tank where the bird can see the fish can reduce boredom. Radio or television stations can be helpful also, but in trying to reduce boredom, it's best not to play the same radio station every day.

Changing anything can make the feather-mutilating problem worse, even if boredom was part of the problem. Sometimes it's better to allow the bird to increase its feather picking while it is adjusting to situations that will provide happiness in the future. At this time a collar to provide a physical barrier against picking can help a bird to adjust to a better situation while changing feather-damaging habits for more appropriate habits.

Toys, Enemies, and Environmental Enrichment

While the role of toys might seem frivolous to some humans, they provide companion parrots with opportunities for decision making: whether to manipulate parts, chew, snuggle, talk, masturbate, or attack. Multiple interesting toys with movable, chewable, and sound-producing parts will help to keep the bird occupied in ways other than grooming, over-grooming, chewing, snapping, or pulling feathers.

The surrogate enemy toy is especially important, for that toy represents a rival or flock member of lower status, and beating up the toy represents the maintenance of status in this highly socially-conscious animal. An African grey parrot that does not have a surrogate enemy toy or a surrogate enemy among household members may be suffering from developmental failure that can lead to feather destructive behavior.

A parrot that is not motivated to chew things other than feathers must be inspired to turn that beak to other elements of the environment. New, unpainted baskets, grapevine wreaths from the hobby store, clean,

new little brooms, cardboard, paper, or bias-cut fabric strips may be introduced to stimulate destructive chewing of external elements rather than feathers.

Change, Change, Change

Changes in the environment can precipitate bouts of feather mutilation in a poorly socialized bird. Prepare the bird to accept and understand change early. Change of residence, moving the cage, rearranging the furniture, remodeling, redecorating, sea-sonal changes in decorations, or in what goes on outside can cause insecurity or even panic.

- When moving or changing residences, try to keep as many things the same as possible. This is not a good time to replace the cage or toys. Try to keep the bird out of the middle of the chaos; try to find someone who will board the bird and cage while things are getting settled. Take the bird on a visit to the new house before it is going to spend the night there.
- When rearranging furniture, remove the bird from the room while moving things around.

- Keep holiday decorations modest around the bird. Put blinking lights and mechanical moving things in a different room or away from where the bird is forced to pay constant attention to them.
- When introducing a parrot to a new cage, try to do it slowly. Although you consider the new cage an improvement, the bird might not. Remember that the cage is a major source of security to the bird and that changing it can really rattle the bird's sense of well-being. If there is a significant negative reaction to a new cage, consider replacing it.

Coordination and Confidence

Good emotional health starts with confidence, and confidence in parrots develops first with physical coordination. Like all infants, baby parrots are occasionally clumsy. A baby bird with an inappropriate wing feather trim, too closely trimmed toenails, and inappropriate perches may be *very* clumsy. This is especially true of heavy-bodied birds such as baby African greys. In the wild, where a fallen baby parrot would be somebody's dinner, baby greys develop extremely sharp toenails as a survival mechanism. In the companion environment, sharp toenails can lead to anxiety by irritating the tender skin of the handler. Failure to allow those sharp toenails,

however, combined with the use of smooth, hard perches, can contribute to frequent falls resulting in damaged or broken feathers. This can, in turn, lead to the development of feather shredding. Add a little unintentional reinforcement or a little bad luck, and we can easily see the development of a behavioral feather-chewing pattern.

As previously discussed, confidence can be enhanced by manipulating height. In some cases that means raising the bird. However, some grey parrots dive down when frightened and may appear calmer and less threatened when housed low, possibly behind a plant or other obstacle designed to improve the bird's sense of safety.

Expect the bird's behavior to change as a result of height manipulations. Especially when treating feather picking related to fearfulness we can expect to see a little aggression appear. While this is not behavior we want to keep, it's a good transitional behavior because it shows that the bird is confident enough to defend territory. A more confident bird is less likely to damage feathers. We can cure the developing aggression later, but unless we see a little territorial behavior, we can assume that this bird has not yet experienced this rite of passage, and this might contribute to feather damage.

Hiding

Some cautious, phobic, or merely shy birds benefit from having places to hide. Often this is provided by covering a part of the top of the cage in a manner that allows the bird to go sit out of sight. Some birds actually need a hide box or a brightly colored fabric tent. Some birds are motivated to sexual behaviors by these "nest sites," which may have to be removed later.

Grooming Wings and Nails

Inappropriate wing and nail grooming can contribute to self-inflicted feather damage, just as cor-rective grooming can assist in recovery. One source of independence for a bird is the ability to move around on its own. The bird's nails should not be so short as to prevent climbing and hanging. Nails that are too long can be just as harmful, since they might get caught in fabric or in cage parts, causing stress as the bird moves around. Sometimes merely correcting the clipping of the nails can precipitate a recovery from feather chewing. Wings should be trimmed to allow the bird to safely flutter down without fear of an uncontrolled landing. A ragged or too-short wing feather trim can contribute to falls and to preening disor-

ders. However, sometimes a ragged trim can be corrected with very sharp scissors. Many birds recover from an incident of self-inflicted feather damage when wing feathers are allowed to grow out completely, then are trimmed only slightly after the bird learns to fly. These birds should not be allowed outside uncontained.

The tip of the beak is also used in climbing and should be long enough and sharp enough to aid in both climbing and hanging. A bird that cannot climb around on the cage or play area without a fear of falling will often feel insecure due to the lack of control over its environment.

Relationships

A well-adjusted grey will form different types of relationships with different "flock members." This often includes forming a matelike bond with a favorite person. There may be a time when the bird seeks to solidify its relationship with this one person to the exclusion of other relationships. Many people will emotionally push the bird away in an attempt to keep the bird from "overbonding." Rather than pulling away, the person should be guiding the bird to learn how to entertain itself and to learn security and self-confidence. Often, the bird will start forming better relationships with other people when it gets a good one going with the favorite person. If this person sets up predictable routines and patterns around which other things can be varied, the bird will be encouraged to be more curious and accepting of change. Paying less attention to the bird during its needy times can cause anxiety and insecurity that sometimes leads to feather destruction.

Changes in the perceived flock can be very upsetting to parrots and also can be hard for owners to control. Introducing new family members—human or animal—can lead to a jealous reaction often based in insecurity. To combat this insecurity, the favorite person can establish a routine before the new member arrives. The old flock member should always be tended to before new additions. It doesn't hurt to praise the established bird after the newcomer gets its attention as well. This most loved person might avoid flaunting a relationship with a significant other in front of the bird. Anytime a parrot is faced with a situation it has no control over, it is going to be more prone to pick feathers.

When a flock member disappears, a sort of mourning period may ensue. Greys form long-term pair bonds. This does not mean that the bird will not form another bond when the original mate disappears, but the bird will miss the companion. This type of stress is commonly associated with self-inflicted feather damage. Maintaining a routine and spending time talking to the bird can sometimes help, even if the bird doesn't want to come out of the cage.

Breeding Stress

Breeding stress is blamed in many cases of feather picking. Someone who owns a bird that damages its own feathers will often be told that the bird "just needs a mate." But there are birds in the wild without mates that most likely do not destroy their own feathers. Many companion birds have found "mates" in their humans. It might be frustrating for the bird that the mate keeps wandering off without it, and this stress might contribute to feather picking. It is unlikely that hormones are the only factor. Giving a feather picker a mate will often result in the feather picker picking its mate or teaching the mate to pick. Breeding time is a stressful time for a bird. Especially those that are actively breeding might pull feathers at this time. The parrot owner must try to ensure that no other elements are adding to the bird's stress.

Accidental Reinforcement

One of the most important but hardest things for a caregiver to do when a beloved bird starts destroying its own feathers is to *not* get excited. The first reaction is often to make a fuss. If the owner runs over and gives the bird attention or scolds it or gives it a treat every time a feather is damaged, then the grey will start pulling feathers to get its owner's attention. If possible, distract the bird *before* it starts picking at feathers. If this is not possible, try to remain neutral. If the owner simply *has* to do something, or if the episode is particularly bad, misting the bird with water while avoiding eye or vocal contact can distract the parrot. Many birds learn to pull feathers when their favorite people respond by begging them to stop.

Devices

Sometimes, a protective device is the only measure capable of preventing self-inflicted damage. Elizabethan collars, sophisticated pop-apart acrylic spheres, or plastic armor are required to eliminate potentially life-threatening, self-inflicted damage to skin. While they should not be considered "cures," like hard acrylic fingernails on dedicated human nail biters, they may be a viable alternative for prevention.

They are especially helpful in the presence of obvious health-related issues such as a staph infection of the skin that is undeniably uncomfortable. These devices, combined with improved behavioral practice upon removal, are necessary and often quite beneficial.

In less difficult cases, body stockings or "teaser" bandanna handkerchief devices designed to encourage the bird to chew on the device rather than to prevent self-destruction may function successfully. Like abstract behavioral techniques, these devices are simply replacements. Like more complex alternatives, they are sometimes needed long-term rather than simply as a transition. Because of the possibility that these fabric devices might get caught on something, they must be used only with careful supervision.

Examination, Distraction, Reinforcement, and Judgments

Examine the environment for newly added elements that might be stressful to the bird such as new art, light fixtures, carpeting, sound-producing clocks, other animals, or provocative humans. Try to protect the bird from loud construction or demolition noises as well as from other loud birds or animals. Consider the possibility that a human or other creatures in the home may be secretly provoking the bird.

Keep a journal to determine exactly when the bird is chewing feathers and exactly what is happening when the feather chewing occurs, including the favorite human's reaction. Once you know when the behavior is occurring, the bird can be distracted to other behaviors, such as showering or exercise before the feather chewing behavior begins.

Of course, at no time should a companion bird be reinforced for engaging in feather-damaging behavior. You must provide for, stimulate, and reinforce other appropriate behaviors. Too much attention

paid to a feather-chewing bird can cause the continuation of the unwanted behaviors.

Owners and caretakers should not be judged or criticized for owning a parrot with chewed feathers. Many caring humans have invested hundreds of dollars and thousands of hours working to help their birds recover from feather destructive behavior. Owning such a parrot is not unlike having a teenager with a habit of nail biting or a fascination with tattoos or piercings. We can't withhold love from a beloved human or bird merely because we don't approve of that individual's personal grooming or ornamentation tastes.

Certainly, this issue defies concrete analysis. Appropriate patterning, a cage that is neither too large nor too small, careful positioning of the cage, gentle handling, full-spectrum lighting, and appropriate diet are only a few elements necessary for a happy, independent parrot. The bird must be healthy and have satisfactory relationships with humans, objects, and locations. It must have an understanding of time and be conditioned to accept changes. A companion parrot requires self-reward and independent habits. The bird must learn that it will not be abandoned, that when people go away, they always come back.

And, even with all systems in place, like health and happiness, everything can change in a New York minute.

Chapter Thirteen
Kids and Critters

African greys and children have tremendous potential to develop highly complimentary relationships, especially an only grey and an only child. Although grey parrots have not been traditionally considered well suited as companions for children, new generations of greys are more likely to adapt well to children and vice versa.

There is also potential for children to damage the sensitive African grey personality, and there is potential for a grey parrot's sharp beak to damage a sensitive child's skin and sense of trust. The best candidates for juvenile African grey owners are kind children at least eight to ten years old. Of course, this advice is highly subjective and depends completely upon the bird and the child. Even some very young children may develop and maintain excellent relationships with African greys. One two-year-old might do very well with a particular grey parrot, and a teenager might not do well with the very same bird.

Careful adult supervision combined with training children to practice step ups and play the towel game can help to ensure a peaceful parrot/child relationship. The bird must demonstrate the same cooperative behaviors with the child as it would with adults. It is especially important to teach a child not to chase a frightened grey parrot that is running away. A child who chases a fearful grey can provoke the fight-or-flight response in the bird, fear biting, defensive aggression, or ongoing panic behaviors. If the bird runs away from the child, train the child to wait until the bird gets to a corner or stopping place, then to approach slowly and give the step-up command, either with a hand-held perch, a bare hand, or a hand covered by a towel in preparation for the towel game. If the bird does not calm down and readily comply with the child's step-up prompt, or if the bird continues in panic mode, instruct the child to seek adult assistance in returning a sense of safety to the bird.

A child must be able to expect help and support from adults in providing adequate care, including annual veterinary exams, for any companion animal. Adults should also regularly examine and trim wing feathers to prevent the loss of the bird from flying-related accidents.

into this category. Jealousy cannot be completely avoided; however, the stress of the situation can be lessened with careful planning.

Providing the parrot with a schedule of attention it can count on can help the bird to feel secure. Months before the baby arrives, set aside a specific time of the day that will be devoted to playing with the bird. Following this pattern as closely as possible after the baby arrives will help the bird know that it isn't being forgotten.

Doll Play

Once the baby arrives, it will be a sudden dominating force in the lives of the parents. This change can be made gradually with the introduction of a baby doll. The expecting parents can first play with the bird, then play with the baby doll. Playing with the bird for a short while after the doll is put away can help the bird realize it is still an important part of their lives. This doll play can be done occasionally at first and then with increasing frequency as the baby's arrival date approaches. The companion grey must understand that it is not to touch the baby and should not learn to expect to interact with the new child.

Using the Name

Once the baby is home, using the bird's name in tandem with the baby's name, as in "*Jaco's Justin*" and "*Justin's Jaco*," can reinforce the connection between the bird and the baby. Once the bird sees that the

Important: Children should be supervised, counseled, and reminded to leave the toilet lid down so that the bird will not drown in the toilet. Likewise, everyone must be vigilant not to leave glasses with liquid where the bird has access to this common drowning hazard. Children must not sleep with these friendly birds and must also be careful not to close them into drawers or behind doors.

Introducing a New Baby to an Established Grey

Any significant changes are best approached gradually if possible. A new baby entering the home falls

baby gets immediate attention when it cries, a grey parrot will probably learn to cry like the baby. Ignoring the bird's crying is probably the best course of action, as any response will reinforce the behavior. The bird will usually stop on its own once the baby stops crying so much.

All Creatures Great and Small

African greys may develop extremely compatible relationships with other pets; they also might develop highly adversarial relationships with them. Like other parrots, African greys often violently defend a bond to a location or a human and jealously abuse others, including pets, that might be perceived as intruders into their territory. While the adjustment period is crucial, some animals will never be able to be together without strict supervision. Here are some guidelines:

• Prepare for a new pet in the home of an established African grey in much the same way as preparing for a new human baby, by telling the bird that the new addition is coming and by sensitively supervising their introduction. You can help the introduction along by introducing the bird first to the accessories needed by the new addition; for instance, let the bird chew on the new dog's collar or the new cat's toys. Use the bird's name in tandem with the new creature: *"Dakar's puppy is coming!"* *"Does the puppy's Dakar want a treat?"*

• Although a grey parrot is much more likely to be killed by a dog than by a cat, caring owners know that their cats must be well socialized as kittens. Some owners even feel that a cat's front claws should be removed if there is a bird in the house. When supervising a new African grey/dog or cat relationship, a carefully timed clap, squirt, or tap on the predator animal's too-interested nose may pattern small pet mammals to discontinue stalking a bird. Always intervene if either animal seems to be trying to chase or attack.

• Always play with the established parrot first. Greys don't usually provoke other animals as much as smaller birds such as *Brotegeris* or *Poicephalus*, but jealousy can do strange things, and a grey can be extremely defensive of favorite people, toys, or locations. If a particular bird decides that harassing the dog is necessary, you can no longer trust that bird with that dog. If the bird has abused the dog repeatedly in the past, some day that dog will defend itself, and the bird might not survive.

• Locating the cage well away from traffic areas is important for a sense of safety. If boisterous animals frequently rush past the grey parrot cage, the bird might develop aggression, fail to talk, begin fraying feathers, or develop thrashing or other problematic behaviors.

- While most African greys share homes well with most cats, ferrets are especially deadly even to larger birds. We do not recommend adding an African grey or any other parrot to a home with a free-roaming ferret.
- African greys can be surprisingly accepting of new birds, although it varies from bird to bird. Many grey parrots cannot be trusted with either larger or smaller birds. Carefully supervise any interaction in which a larger animal interacts with a smaller one, especially if the African grey is the larger animal. African greys can be a threat to smaller creatures such as insects, spiders, lizards, reptiles, mice, hamsters, and gerbils.

Chapter Fourteen
Gone, Gone Grey

In the past, a lost grey parrot probably wouldn't go to strangers. Because of their cautious natures, it was a little more difficult to recapture an African grey than other, bolder types of parrots. As more and more babies come up through well-socialized channels, however, we can expect this to change.

Timing and Tracking

Of course, prevention of flyaways is preferred, but in case of accidental escape, prompt action can mean more success in recovering the bird. Work quickly. Try to keep the bird in sight. Have several spotters in place so that if the bird flies, you'll see where it goes, and if it decides to go to someone, someone will be there. A hand-fed New World parrot will often go to almost any human by dark the first or second evening it is out. Many African parrots are so shy that they often will stay outside, terrified, hungry, and alone in the dark, rather than go to a stranger. This can work to their advantage if they are waiting for just the right person, and if they remain still and quiet to avoid attracting predators.

By the second or third day, a lost hand-fed grey parrot should be very, very hungry, very thirsty, and very ready to find a friendly person. While this can ensure the bird's survival, there is no guarantee that this means the bird will be returned. Humans who find a bird are sometimes tempted to keep it. Rescuers might be judgmental about an owner who doesn't trim a bird's wing feathers. It is, therefore, important for the owner to immediately report a missing bird to police and animal control and to offer a reward for the bird's return. This demonstrates the owner's honorable intentions and dedication toward the bird. It establishes that the bird is lost property to be legally claimed.

Remember, not everyone who finds a lost companion parrot is honest. It's not uncommon for a less-than-scrupulous stranger holding a lost African grey for ransom to have an exaggerated idea of the bird's actual material value. I like to mention on the flyer that the bird is somehow imperfect, and therefore, not especially valuable. With an

hates most will bring the bird down sooner than the presence of food or the most-beloved person. Especially if the bird is very jealous and the favorite person is expressing affection to the most hated rival, an African grey parrot will come down more quickly because of jealousy than hunger. Most greys will climb down rather than fly down, but if you're encouraging the bird to fly to you, be sure the wind is at your back when looking up at the bird as it must take off into the wind.

If you have to climb to get close enough to reach the bird, be sure to take a pillowcase with you. It's hard enough to hold onto an angry, flighted African grey, much less climb with one. Just tie the pillowcase in a knot to contain the bird and lower it carefully to a helper on the ground. If you must climb, don't use metal ladders around power lines. Electrocution is the most common cause of death or serious injury in a pet bird recapture accident. The safest possible climbing accessory is a cherry picker, a large piece of equipment that comes with a professional operator. In the case of a grey parrot recapture, the bird will usually go only to a familiar person, so that is the person who must go up the tree or ladder or cherry picker to retrieve the bird.

Avoid the use of water hoses. Not only do hoses have an extremely short range, and it's often difficult to

older bird I might say that the bird is known to attack or that it has daily medical needs.

Especially, *don't give up!* Keep looking. A bird doesn't just disappear.

When You Know Where the Bird Is

If the bird is in a high, inaccessible place, you can sometimes lure it down with a like bird, food, or jealousy. Sometimes the presence of the person the African grey parrot

Checklist for Finding a Flown-Away Bird

When you don't know where the bird is, the recapture project becomes first a public relations job:

1. Immediately report the loss to police so that if the bird is found and anyone holding the bird won't relinquish it, the police may intervene. You must be able to prove ownership, possibly with a recorded band number, registered DNA configuration, microchipping, photos, and veterinary or behaviorist records.

2. Call local humane societies, animal control authorities, local bird dealers, avian veterinarians, groomers, recapture and lost pet services.

3. Walk around the neighborhoods the bird flew from and where it might have flown to and talk with anyone willing to talk, especially children on playgrounds, for this is where the birds are often attracted.

4. Occasionally blow an athletic whistle then listen for a response. Don't forget to look in all directions, as the bird will probably circle as soon as it figures out it's lost.

5. Place ads in local newspapers (especially publications people can pick up for free), on the Internet, and on church and grocery store bulletin boards.

6. Make a flyer with a photo or a likeness of the bird. Prepare a white original so that it can be easily copied onto brightly colored paper. Use a different paper color each time the flyer is reprinted. If the recapture process lasts awhile, signs should be reposted after bad weather, and a new color will help people to understand that the search is still "fresh," and they should call if they see the bird. Don't use staples when posting fliers on poles that someone will have to climb.

7. The flyer should contain a contact phone number, an alternate contact number, and a local landmark nearest to where the bird flew away.

8. Include any identifying characteristics, such as a missing toe or banding on a particular leg, but don't reveal the band number, so that that information can be used to differentiate between a person who really has your bird and an unscrupulous person who might be pretending to have your bird.

9. Be sure to mention small rewards available for any information leading to the location of the bird and a sizable reward for the bird's return.

10. Be sure to include the line "This notice will be removed promptly when the bird is found." It might save you many phone calls, including one (and a fine) from a code compliance inspector. Then don't forget to take the flyers down immediately upon recovering the bird. It's only polite, and in some places you may be fined if you do not take them down.

LOST PET BIRD

Virgil, an **AFRICAN GREY PARROT**

Lost on September 7, 2008
near Sheridan & Yale
in Lakewood, CO

A shy bird that probably won't go
to strangers, Virgil's feathers are
chewed revealing down on the breast

Virgil requires maintenance medication

*Substantial Reward for
the bird's return*

*Small Rewards for any
information leading to
his return*

**Call Mattie Sue at 333-555-1234 if you see
A LARGE GRAY BIRD WITH A RED TAIL**

Marty's Choice

Marty was vital, active, and wheelchair-bound. He was the long-time owner of an African grey parrot. One summer morning as he emerged from the shower, Marty discovered that his wife had left the back door wide open when she went to work. On that particular morning, Marty had taken Ben, his companion grey, into the shower with him. Turning the corner to the kitchen with Ben perched on his lap, they both saw the open back door, and at that exact moment, the door behind them blew shut with a loud "Bang!"

Ben, who was scheduled for a wing trim that very day, was startled and flew out the back door. Marty, wet, dripping, and dressed only in a towel draped over his lap, followed out onto the patio in his rolling chair. There was Ben, perched in the lowest fork of a young crabapple tree beside the picnic table. He was only inches out of Marty's reach, clicking and pinpointing his eys, obviously enjoying his sunny freedom.

Marty took no time making his decision. Hoping that his neighbors weren't watching, he chose his bird over modesty. Pulling himself almost upright, Marty flipped the towel over his errant grey friend, pulled him from the fork of the tree, and wheeled, naked, back to the house with an angry grey parrot wrapped in a towel.

Ben would be on time for his wing-trimming appointment, and Marty would be avoiding his neighbors for a few days.

---

get close enough to the bird even to get it wet, but grey parrots can be excellent fliers, even when wet. It's highly unlikely that a good-flying African grey can be prevented from flying with water from a garden hose, and the strong pressure of water from a firefighter's hose could kill the bird. On the other hand, those huge "Supersoaker" water guns can shoot a stream of water up to 50 feet (15 m). The bird can sometimes be "herded" down to lower and lower places with the water gun, but this is tricky and not recommended for African greys unless there is no other alternative, for example, if the bird is in a very inaccessible place. With this technique you run the risk of causing the bird to be even more wary and difficult to trap. It could also cause long-term behavioral implications in a very reactionary bird.

Although capturing a free-flying hand-fed African grey might be as easy as walking up and saying "Step up!" recapturing an experienced, human-wary feral African grey can seem a gargantuan task.

The food dish is lowered on a movable shelf until the bird must enter the cage to get it, and a human waiting out of sight pulls the door closed with a string.

Traps

The easiest way to capture a good-flying, human-shy bird is to first establish food dependency, then trap the bird. A trap can be easily made from a manufactured parrot cage lying on its back with a movable wire rack that can be placed at the top opening to the cage.

First, place food on a white dish on top of the cage. Each day, move the shelf lower into the cage. Within a few days, the bird will have to go into the cage to get the food, and you can pull the door closed, trapping the bird inside. It is also helpful to have a like species bird within the trapping apparatus as a lure.

Theft

Because hand-fed greys often relish cuddling, and because they are frequently accessible for handling by the public in retail settings, babies are the most likely stolen African grey parrots. Greys appeal to both amateur and professional bird thieves because they are quiet, easy to snuggle into a coat lining or under a shirt, and very valuable for their relatively small size. This can be especially tragic if the baby bird is being hand-fed or has other special needs.

Breeders and retailers must be watchful when unfamiliar groups come to look at babies. A typical theft scenario often involves one person, sometimes a child, making a scene or requiring assistance at a location away from where the birds are kept while an accomplice puts a baby bird inside a garment. Baby grey parrots should be accessible to unfamiliar individuals only with clean hands and with supervision.

Chapter Fifteen
Basic Breeding

Aviculture is as much art as science. Most published information on housing and nest box styles are generalizations based on what has worked for other breeders. Therefore, it's important to know what has worked specifically for other breeders of African greys. Anyone seriously considering breeding these wonderful, sensitive birds needs comprehensive information from experienced breeders of African grey parrots. In addition to birds, you will need equipment, information, and resources for emergency advice in place well before the arrival of the first egg.

Rick Jordan's *Parrot Incubation Procedures* (1990) and *Parrots: Hand-Feeding and Nursery Management* (with Howard Voren, 1992) provide invaluable instructions, even for those who plan to let the parents do most of the initial work. More germane to this text, Rick Jordan also coauthored a book on African parrots in aviculture with Jean Pattison, *The African Queen*. These books should be read and reread before even one pair of grey parrots is set up to breed.

Housing

Wild-caught grey parrots might prefer spacious flights, but today's captive-raised, former pet greys will probably appreciate a cage small enough to provide security, but large enough to move around freely. Of course, longer horizontal dimension is more important than height. Minimum suggested dimensions are 4 feet long, 3 feet tall, and 2 to 3 feet wide (122 cm × 91 cm × 61–91 cm). Smaller cages may lead to heartbreaking results, such as injury to the mate, broken eggs, or injured chicks.

The Nest Box

L- or Z-shaped nest boxes typically work best for greys. Some chew wood during breeding season, so the boxes should be made of thick plywood and regularly inspected for new holes. There should be an access door for checking eggs and removing babies.

The nest box should be outside the cage with the bird's access hole inside and the inspection door outside the cage. Most pairs will prefer a box that is entered near the top of

the cage with a quiet and tranquil view. The access hole should be about 3 inches (7.6 cm) across. If the birds want the hole larger, they will enlarge it by chewing the wood.

Pine shavings or paper-based litters are good nesting material. Corncob and crushed walnut shells can grow molds that are particularly harmful to the chicks. Oils in cedar shavings are potentially toxic. Paper from most paper shredders is too long and can become wrapped around the birds' legs or necks. Use nontoxic glue to adhere cork to the bottom of the nest box if the parents like to completely remove bedding from the nest cavity. This will provide chicks with an appropriate surface needed to prevent "spraddle leg."

Obtaining a Pair

Of course, no breeding can be accomplished without a compatible male and female bird. If you're work-ing with former pets, look for sweet and well-adjusted birds as there's a good chance that these characteristics will be passed on to the babies. Cherished pets are more likely to beget cherished baby pets, but there are some problems associated with setting up human-bonded African greys to breed. Among other things, even though the female birds are usually less particular, a companion male grey parrot that is extremely bonded to humans may be unwilling to mate with a mere bird.

Then there's the matter of availability. Domestically bred birds are usually more expensive than imported birds unless they are, for some reason, unsuitable as pets. Grey parrots with behavioral issues such as aggression, phobias, or feather plucking are much more easily acquired than confident-but-placid, bird-bonded, talking birds in perfect feather.

Unfortunately, the easiest birds to find are exactly the ones that should not be bred. The future of greys in pet-oriented aviculture depends on producing birds whose temperament is suitable for life in captivity. Birds that are poor pets should not be bred to produce more birds that are poor pets.

Gender and Bonding

While there are some differences in appearance between male and female greys, anyone pairing birds for breeding needs to have gender determined either by DNA or surgical sexing. DNA sexing can be easily accessed by mail with a sample kit. A drop of blood is collected from a trimmed toenail, then sent to be analyzed. You'll know if it's a she or vice versa within a week. This method is much easier on the bird than surgical sexing, although the bird might have a sore toe for a day or two.

In surgical sexing, the veterinarian puts the parrot under anesthesia and uses an endoscope to look inside. By looking inside, the veterinarian will be able to actually visualize the status of the bird's reproductive organs; however, there are risks involved with general anesthesia, including death.

Two birds of opposite gender do not automatically make a bonded pair. The birds must be willing to bond with each other. Love-at-first-sight pairs tend to be the most successful. If one of the birds can't stand the other, there's little chance of that bird changing its mind. Look for an alternate mate. As previously mentioned, some hand-fed birds may be so human-oriented that they will be reluctant to bond with a parrot.

Special Needs of Breeding Parrots

Diet. Breeding parrots require a better diet than parrot companions. Any parrots that breed regularly, especially if they have two or three clutches yearly, will probably need additional Vitamin E and calcium. Any other dietary supplements should be evaluated and approved by an avian veterinarian.

Lighting. Full-spectrum lighting enhances productivity. Lighting can be timed so that birds are provided with 12 hours of daylight and 12 hours of night, although variable lighting cycles may increase productivity.

Grooming. Grey parrots often have very sharp toenails. "Needle toes" can put holes in eggs, so it's a good idea to groom the nails before the birds go to nest.

Privacy. Greys are often very private breeders. Copulation and related behaviors are seldom seen by humans. Many pairs appear to copulate only in the nest box and will not produce if they are disturbed too often.

Stimulating Breeding Behaviors

While some breeders find they have no trouble at all stimulating breeding by merely feeding an exceptional diet, some aviculturists report that they must use environmental manipulations to stimulate breeding behaviors.

- Add shortened "winter" days for about three weeks before breeding is desired.
- Add an artificial rainy season by increasing showers when breeding is desired.
- Change the diet, possibly providing an artificial harvest period where food is suddenly more abundant.

- Move the cage and/or nest box, or just take the birds for a ride in the car.
- Consider changing the direction the nest hole faces.
- Fill the nest box with shavings so that the birds will be stimulated by removing them.

Eggs

As laying begins, the birds should be given as much food as they will eat, especially calcium- and protein-rich foods. The hen usually lays two to four eggs at two-day intervals.

As mentioned, the birds must be provided as much privacy as possible at this time. It may be difficult to socialize the birds to allow nest box inspection. While some breeders advise not disturbing birds on eggs, we believe that good husbandry can save more eggs and more chicks if the birds have been conditioned to allow daily inspection of the nest box. Some pairs do not allow this and there's a chance of breaking eggs if disturbed. Again, it's best to know your birds and accommodate their specific needs.

Once a fertile egg is five to seven days old, blood vessels can be seen by light passing through the egg (candling). Incubation typically lasts 24 to 26 days, although it can be delayed as long as four or five days if the birds do not begin sitting immediately. It's possible to candle eggs without removing them from the nest box, but only if the parents are out of the box. Otherwise the parents could break the eggs and injure the keeper.

Once the eggs have hatched, parents need plenty of nutritious soft food. Their caloric intake will increase dramatically. Vegetables, cooked beans, and moistened whole-grain bread are good foods that can be increased in quantity. (This is NOT a good time to try to change the diet!) As chicks grow larger, more and more calories will be consumed by parents and fed to the babies.

Care and Feeding of Chicks

If possible, chicks should be left with their parents for the first ten days. When parents feed chicks, they incorporate digestive enzymes that enable the chicks to better absorb and utilize nutrients. Very young chicks have no ability to regulate body temperature and are very sensitive to temperature changes. They can become chilled during the time required for hand-feeding.

Baby parrots, especially greys, must be removed from the parents at an age young enough that they are not traumatized by the transition. Our experience has been that the chicks adapt easily to the new "parent" if removed from the nest by the time they are three weeks old. Leaving the babies in the nest longer is possible but some individual babies may not adapt easily to handfeeding.

Alternatively, you might consider "coparenting": handling babies over ten days old every day and returning them to the nest box. This is especially risky with a sensitive pair, but reportedly, chicks and very gregarious parents might thrive with such technique.

Temperature and Humidity

Check for published temperature and humidity guidelines, but adjustments should be made for the individual birds involved. A brooder with controls for temperature and humidity can save a great deal of worry and guesswork. However, many babies have been raised without sophisticated equipment.

Temperature. For babies not yet covered with fuzzy gray down, the temperature should be between 90 and 95°F (32–35°C). If babies are shivering or huddled together, the temperature should be raised slightly. If they are panting, the temperature should be lowered. Chicks should look comfortable. The more babies being kept together, the less added heat will be required. As chicks develop, the temperature should gradually be reduced. Once the chicks are feathered, they should do quite well at 78°F (25°C).

Humidity. Moisture in the air should be kept around 60 percent for most young chicks. It should be

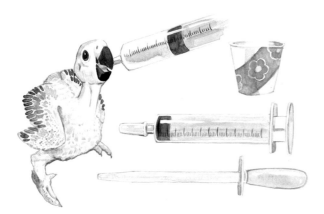

A paper cup, syringe, and pipette are easy-to-use hand-feeding tools.

increased if the baby is showing signs of dehydration such as red skin. Red skin may also mean that the hand-feeding formula is too dry or that the baby has developed an infection. A consultation with an avian veterinarian may be necessary if a chick is observably red for more than a day.

Housing Chicks

Until they are ready to get up and start moving around on their own, chicks should be provided with a nest that allows enough room for all of the chicks, but not much extra. The bones in their legs are not hard at this point and may become deformed if the baby can't keep them tucked under. Bedding should be something that the little parrots can get traction on. Cloth diapers work well. Washcloths and hand towels are not smooth enough, and babies get their toenails caught, with adverse effect.

Bedding should be changed several times daily. With only a few babies, a paper towel can be placed over the cloth and replaced between the times that the cloth is replaced. Paper towels should not be used by themselves because they do not absorb as much as the diaper and get too cold when they are not completely dry. Especially in dry climates, moisture retained by the cloth can be beneficial by boosting humidity and keeping babies from drying out.

As the babies get older, they can be moved to a container that allows them to move around. They will be too old for a brooder but may still need added heat. A 10-gallon (38 L) aquarium is easily converted as a brooder with shredded paper in the bottom and a heating pad under one end. Privacy is very important, as is the ability to peek out. Drape a towel over one end so that the babies can either hide in the security of the towel or come out and look around.

At this age the babies put all kinds of things in their mouths and can swallow them. Bedding should not be easily swallowed and not harmful if it is. Wood shavings are not acceptable, as they can puncture the thin skin over the baby's crop. Many organic litters can carry spores of fungus and bacteria that can become active when there are soiled droppings. Paper from a shredder is useful if the strips are not more than half a sheet long. Longer strips can get wrapped around the chick's legs or neck.

Diet

There are many formulated diets to choose from, and they are not all created equal. By talking with local avian veterinarians and bird breeders, you can find out what kinds of formulated diets are available in the area and which of those is best for grey parrots. The labels of a few of these diets can then be compared and a decision made as to which brand to try. The breeder should choose the formula before the chicks are hatched.

Instructions for use always come with the package of formula. Many breeders have ways of "doctoring" the formula, but this is not recommended. Changing formulas is also not recommended unless directed by a veterinarian.

Hand-feeding

There are several hand-feeding tools to choose from and entire books have been written on this subject as well as on weaning the chicks. Hand-feeding is always best learned by example.

Preparing the formula: Hand-feeding formula should be mixed according to its specific instructions to a consistency easily delivered by the method chosen and easily digested by the chick. The temperature should be brought to 104°F (40°C). Temperatures exceeding 43°F (6°C) could scald the crop, so an accurate thermometer is essential. A hot water bath can be used to adjust the temperature. Heating formula in the microwave creates "hot spots," which can cause crop burn and death.

Spoon-feeding: One of the most preferred ways of administering the food is spoon-feeding. A spoon is used with the sides bent in a manner resembling the parents' lower beak, then filled with food with the end allowed to rest inside the baby's beak. The baby's feeding motion enables food to fall from the spoon into the mouth, and the baby is allowed to take as much as it wants at a time. This method most closely resembles the way chicks are fed by parents. It also requires the hand-feeder to spend more time with each

individual youngster, an especially wonderful behavioral advantage for grey parrots.

Feeding devices: When using a syringe or pipette, an understanding of basic anatomy is required. The trachea opens at the base of the tongue. The esophagus is behind the trachea. In the throat the esophagus curves to the right and goes into the L-shaped crop. The baby bird must hold its breath or breathe out while the food passes over the trachea and into the crop. For the most part, this is reflexive; however, keeping the food in the mouth for too long can result in the baby needing to breathe and aspirating some of the formula. Knowing that the esophagus curves over to the right side of the bird, many hand-feeders like to hold the syringe or pipette to the left side of the bird's beak.

Sometimes, a hand-feeder will be nervous about the baby aspirating and as a result, will tube- or gavage-feed babies. With this method a tube or feeding "needle" is inserted into the chick's crop. The food passes directly into the crop without touching the baby's mouth. This method is less natural than other hand-feeding techniques discussed here. It is an invasive procedure and does not allow the little parrot to become accustomed to the taste and feeling of food in its mouth. This is a controversial technique that probably should be considered only for emergency situations.

Nurturing time: The amount of time spent with each baby is very important. The idea behind pulling the chicks from their nurturing parents is for them to associate nurturing with human contact. Nurturing takes time; this is part of the purpose of hand-feeding. If there is too little time to cuddle each baby at feeding time, be sure to make time for cuddling later.

Feeding schedule: The chick's crop should be filled to bulging but not distended. The baby should be fed again when the crop is empty. The amount of time between feedings depends upon the age of the chick and the amount of food the crop will hold as well as how thick the formula is and what kind of formula is used. The time between feedings should gradually increase as the bird steadily gains weight. Any sudden increase in the time it takes for the crop to empty could indicate a problem.

The feeding response: A regurgitation response is stimulated when a chick grabs a parent's beak and pumps in a rapid up-and-down motion. Baby greys also share food and practice this behavior with each other and can be encouraged to do it with the hand-feeder's fingers. This behavior is analogous to suckling by human babies. As with young humans, the urge to solicit food is not always connected to the lack of or presence of food in the crop or stomach. While children can suck their thumbs, baby birds cannot fill this need on their own. You must spend time allowing the babies to "suck" on fingers or feeding instruments so that the chick can fulfill this need. Allowing the little grey to engage in this behavior without actually being fed is in no way teasing; it probably stimulates a feeling of security, similar to a child sucking its thumb.

Weaning

Preparation for weaning actually starts when the chick hatches and gets its first meal. Neglecting to consider this can make the weaning stage notoriously stressful and difficult for many young birds. Parent greys and other parrots do not produce a special food for the baby birds as do some other bird species. From the very start, the baby is allowed to sample the different flavors and textures of foods regularly eaten by the parents. These experiences are imprinted in the young bird and are what the weaning bird draws on when it begins feeding itself. A young bird that has reached the age of weaning, having experienced only the flavor and texture of hand-feeding formula, must overcome the effects of its sensory deprivation before it can learn to eat independently.

While you cannot chew up food for baby parrots and mix it with digestive enzymes the way a parent bird does, you can provide this early sensory stimulation. At four or five weeks of age, the bird should have the appearance of being fully feathered from a top view even though it may still be missing many of its body feathers. The chick will be producing

enough of its own enzymes to be able to digest small amounts of crushed or minced vegetables. The vegetables should be wet and at the same temperature as the hand-feeding formula. Initially, you can put one or two pinches of food in the bird's mouth while eliciting the feeding response. You can then give the baby its formula as usual. The pinch of food will not digest as quickly as the formula but should be gone within 24 hours. The baby should be hand-fed as if the solid food were not there. If the solid food is not gone by the next day, the baby may not be old enough to handle it yet. You should wait five to seven days before trying again. If the solid food is easily digested, the baby can be fed solid food once daily. The amount can be gradually increased as the baby becomes stronger and more able to digest the food.

Young greys will increasingly visualize food as weaning nears. Showing the solid food to the baby as it is brought to its mouth helps the chick learn to associate the appearance of the food with eating it.

As soon as chicks are walking around and exploring their environment, they should be provided with low dishes of food. The babies will play with the food and drag it around. Gradually, they will begin actually eating increasing amounts of it. Eventually, they will refuse hand-feeding formula on a regular basis, although even a fully weaned bird may accept warm formula-like food on an occasional basis.

Glossary

Note: Please note that the following definitions set forth the meanings of these words as they are used specifically in this text. They are not intended to be full and complete definitions.

adaptive behaviors: learned behaviors that increase the bird's chances of surviving by producing more offspring.

adapted: having adjusted to the environment in a positive manner.

Ailanthus: "trees of heaven," so named for a Moluccan word meaning, "tree that grows up to the sky"; weed tree common in older urban cities in the United States. Soft, easy-to-grip branches well suited as African grey parrot perches.

aggression: hostile nipping, biting, or chasing.

allofeeding: mutual feeding or simulated mutual feeding. One of several behaviors related to breeding.

allopreening: mutual preening or simulated mutual preening, as in a human scratching a parrot's neck.

altricial: a bird that is helpless upon hatching and must be cared for by its parents.

aviary birds: birds that live in captivity, but in a bird-identified setting in which they do not interact on a regular basis with humans.

baby days: a young parrot's first, impressionable weeks in the new home, an idyllic period before the baby bird's instincts for independence, dominance, and exploration develop. *See also:* honeymoon period.

band: coded metal device placed around a bird's leg for identification purposes.

beaking: testing the feel of the beak on various substances, including skin by a baby parrot.

behavioral environment: behavioral conditions, especially redundant behaviors including habits, present in the bird and in individuals around the bird.

bite: use of the parrot's beak in a manner intended to cause damage or injury.

blood feather: unopened immature feather that is completely or partially covered by a bluish/white membrane indicating that the feather is currently supplied with blood.

body language: nonvocal communication involving posturing, displaying, or otherwise signaling an individual's feelings or intentions.

bond: the connection with another bird, a human, object, or location that a bird exhibits and defends.

boredom: stress caused in companion parrots by a lack of access to activities that they would be instinctually suited to experience, including wild and self-rewarding companion pastimes.

breeding-related behaviors: behaviors with a source related to breeding habits in the wild such as chewing, emptying cavities, hiding in dark places, allopreening, allofeeding, masturbating, copulating, and aggression at the nest site (cage).

cage bound: so fixated on an unchanging environment that any change stimulates either aggression or fearfulness in a captive bird.

cavity-breeding behaviors: breeding-related behaviors of parrots including chewing, emptying cavities, fondness for small spaces, peeking out, and aggression at the nest site.

chasing: to drive away by pursuing.

chewing: breeding-related behavior involving destruction of wood or other shredable environmental elements.

clutch: siblings hatching from the same group of eggs.

command: a prompt or instruction given to stimulate a behavior.

companion parrot: a parrot that lives as a companion to humans.

contour: a layer of covering feathers as in the gray and green feathers covering the bird's down.

cue: a word or group of words established to stimulate certain behaviors.

dander: powder formed when discarded sheaths are removed from new feathers or powder that is contained in certain down feathers that is released when the bird preens.

developmental period: a period of rapid behavioral development wherein a parrot may demonstrate tendencies for dominance, independence, aggression, and panic. *See also:* terrible twos.

diarrhea: abnormal droppings that include undigested food in the feces or do not have three distinct parts. Diarrhea is accompanied by weight loss in the bird.

dominance: control, enforcing individual will over others.

down: the small fuzzy feathers next to the body that are normally covered by coverts.

drama: any activity that brings an exciting response, either positive or negative.

eye contact: the act of maintaining an eye-to-eye gaze.

family: category ranking above genus.

feather cyst: one or more feathers growing under the skin causing an uncomfortable abscess.

feather destructive behavior: self-inflicted feather damage involving damaging any part of the feather including the edges or the center shaft or rachis.

feather picking: used here to refer to any kind of self-inflicted feather damage including shredding, snapping, or plucking feathers from the follicles.

feather plucking: pulling feathers from the follicles.

feather shredding: self-inflicted damage to the edge of the barbs of the contour feathers, sometimes giving the feathers a hairlike appearance.

feather snapping: self-inflicted feather damage involving breaking off the center shaft or rachis.

feather tracts: symmetrical lines on bird's body where feathers grow in; especially visible on neonatal parrots.

feces: excreted solid waste, usually "wormlike," which can be differentiated from urates and liquid urine.

fight-or-flight response: instinctual, automatic reaction to real or perceived danger.

fledge: the act of learning to fly in order to leave the nest.

flock/flock members: as it applies to a companion bird, human companions sharing a home with a captive parrot.

forage: the search for and consumption of food.

free feeding: allowing access to food at all times.

gavage: a tube designed to deliver food or medicine directly into the crop, or the act of doing so.

genus: a group of related species, usually sharing basic morphological and behavioral characteristics.

grooming: the process of having the companion parrot's wing feathers trimmed, nails cut or filed, and beak shaped, if necessary.

habit: redundant behavior that has become a fixed part of the bird's behavior.

hand-fed: a parrot that as a neonate was fed by humans rather than birds.

handling techniques: methods used by humans to stimulate and maintain successful tactile interactions with companion parrots.

honeymoon period: a young parrot's first, impressionable weeks in the new home, an idyllic period before the baby bird's instinct for dominance and exploration develop. *See also:* baby days.

hookbill: a parrot.

human/mate: the human companion chosen by the bird to fill the role of mate. The bird will perform courtship displays for this person and protect this person as it would a mate of the same species.

imprint: to form a parentlike bond with the initial nurturer as a result of having been removed from the nest so early that the bird is confused as to what its parents look like. An imprinted bird will treat humans in the same manner it would treat another bird.

independence: improvising and enjoying self-rewarding behaviors.

juvenile: fully weaned, but immature grey parrots. Also, behaviors unrelated to nesting or breeding.

keel bone: the flat bone below the bird's crop that is attached perpendicular to the sternum.

language: vocal communication wherein multiple individuals use the same groups of sounds to convey the same meaning.

maladaptive: behaviors that decrease the bird's ability to function in its environment.

Manzanita: commercially available hardwood branches, which, in small sizes, are suitable as perches for adult grey parrots with no gripping or perching problems.

mandible: the lower beak or horny protuberance with which the bird bites against the inside of the maxilla.

mantling: wing outstretching happiness behavior as described in falconry.

masticate: to chew, as in this case, with the beak.

mate: the individual to whom the parrot is primarily bonded. *See also:* human/mate.

maxilla: the upper beak; the notched protuberance that gives the hookbill its name.

mimicking: copying modeled behavior, especially vocalizations.

model: a learning process by which one individual demonstrates behavior for another.

molt: the cyclical shedding and replacing of feathers.

neonate: a baby parrot that cannot yet sustain itself by eating food independently. In the case of baby greys, these birds are usually being hand-fed.

nest/nesting: the act of constructing a structure for the purpose of reproduction.

nest box: a human-constructed box for bird nesting.

nipping: an accidental, unintentional, or nonaggressive pinch not intended to cause damage.

normal: the original animal that occurs wild; not a color mutation (pied, lutino, or albino).

parrot: a hookbill; a bird with a notched maxilla, a mallet-shaped tongue, and four toes (two facing front and two facing back).

patterning: stimulating an individual to repeat behaviors through the process of repeatedly drilling the behavior.

pecking order: the hierarchy of dominance within a group of birds or their companions.

phobic: having an irrational or unexplainable fear.

pinch: a behavior designed to get a human's attention where the bird takes that person's skin in its beak and squeezes hard enough to cause pain, but not hard enough to break the skin.

polymer fume fever: the condition that can kill a bird that is exposed to fumes from Teflon heated to 500°F.

preen: to groom the feathers, as with "combing" and "zipping" them with the beak.

prompt: a cue, here used for the physical cue to cause the bird to step up.

psittacine: relating to any parrot.

Psittacus: a genus of African grey parrots.

quarantine: enforced isolation for the prevention of disease transmission.

reactive: to quickly revert to instinctual reactions such as aggression or fear.

recapture: to apprehend or recover possession of a parrot that has flown away.

regurgitate: voluntary or involuntary production of partially digested food from the crop. *See also:* allofeeding.

reinforce: rewarding a behavior that we wish to become habitual.

reprimand: punishment; action intended to discourage a behavior.

rescue: fortuitous removal from frightening circumstances.

rival: a competitor, one who competes for territory, reinforcement, or reward.

roaming: unsupervised explorations away from approved cage or play areas.

roost: the place where a bird usually sleeps.

self-mutilation: self-induced damage to the skin.

self-rewarding behavior: an activity that is enacted solely for the pleasure of doing it.

sexual behavior: self-rewarding breeding-related behavior.

sexual maturity: the period during which breeding-related behaviors become prominent in the bird's overall behavior.

signaling: anything—vocalization, tapping, or other body language—that warns, alerts, or telegraphs an intention or apparent impending behavior. A vocalization that falls short of true language.

species: subgenus; related groups of individuals that share common biological characteristics.

spraddle leg: a deformity that prevents normal use of any of the joints of the leg, usually causing the leg to bend outward.

status: positioning related to dominance within the pecking order.

step-up: practice of giving the step-up command with the expectation that the bird will perform the behavior.

sternum: the breastbone from which the keel bone protrudes.

stress: any stimulus, especially fear or pain, that inhibits normal psychological, physical, or behavioral balance.

submission: allowing another creature to demonstrate dominant status.

subspecies: a subdivision of species, especially by color or geographical characteristics.

substratum: material placed in the bottom of the bird's cage or play area to contain mess and droppings; plural, substrata.

Sumac: a small, sparsely branching weed tree found in pastures and adjoining land throughout most of the United States. Sumac is not poisonous, but rather is a common food source for many native species of birds. It is a little too soft to be a good perch for African greys except as a transitional treatment for failure to chew.

teaser: a skin or feather-protection device designed to attract chewing behaviors to itself rather than preventing access to feathers.

terrible twos: a behavioral period wherein the bird's instincts for dominance, independence, and aggression are first manifest. *See also*: developmental period.

"the thunderbolt": a parrot's tendency to be smitten by love at first sight.

tools: an implement that is manipulated to accomplish a particular function.

toxin: any substance that causes illness or death through exposure to it.

toy: any tool for producing self-rewarding behavior.

trap: a device used to recapture a free-flying bird.

urates: nitrogenous wastes; the solid "white" part of a bird's excrement.

urine: clear, colorless liquid part of the bird's excrement.

vent: cloaca.

vocabulary: words or elements comprising a language.

weaned: capable of eating a variety of foods independent of help or supervision.

window of opportunity: a finite period during which something can be accomplished, a period of time during which behavior can be changed.

Resources

Organizations

The African Parrot Society
wingscentral.org

American Federation of Aviculture
P.O. Box 91717
Austin, TX 78709-1717

British Columbia Avicultural Society
11784 Ninth Avenue
North Delta, British Columbia
V4C 3H6
Canada

Canadian Parrot Association
32 Dronmore Court
Willowdale, Ontario
M2R 2H5
Canada

International Aviculturists Society
P.O. Box 2232
LaBelle, FL 33975

National Parrot Rescue and
 Preservation Foundation
parrotfestival.org

Oasis Parrot Sanctuary
P.O. Box 3104
Scottsdale, AZ 85271

World Parrot Trust
P.O. Box 34114
Memphis, TN 38184

Books

Athan, Mattie Sue. *Guide to a Well-Behaved Parrot, 3rd Ed*. Hauppauge, NY: Barron's Educational Series, Inc., 2008.

———. *Guide to Companion Parrot Behavior*. Hauppauge, NY: Barron's Educational Series, Inc., 1999.

———. *Parrots: A Complete Pet Owner's Manual*. Hauppauge, NY: Barron's Educational Series, Inc., 2002.

———. *The Second-Hand Parrot*. Hauppauge, NY: Barron's Educational Series, Inc., 2002.

Bergman, Petra. *Feeding Your Pet Bird*. Hauppauge, NY: Barron's Educational Series, Inc., 1993.

Forshaw, Joseph M. *Parrots of the World*. Neptune, NJ: TFH Publications, Inc., 1977.

Gonzales, Fran. *African Greys*. Yorba Linda, CA: Neon Pet Publications, 1996.

Greeson, Linda. *Parrot Personalities*. Fruitland Park, FL: Greeson's Baby Parrots, 1993.

Harrison, Greg J. and Linda R. Harrison. *Clinical Avian Medicine and Surgery*. Philadelphia, PA: W. B. Saunders and Co., 1986.

Jupiter, Tony and Mike Parr. *Parrots: A Guide to Parrots of the World*. New Haven, CT: Yale University Press, 1998.

Paper and Online Magazines

The AFA Watchbird
afawatchbird@earthlink.net

Bird Talk
P.O. Box 6050
Mission Viejo, CA 92690

Companion Parrot Handbook
companionparrot.com

Good Bird Magazine
goodbirdinc.com/magazine.html

Parrot Chronicles
parrotchronicles.com

Wikipedia
Wikipedia.com

Index